WATERFRONT

THE ILLUSTRATED MARITIME STORY OF GREATER VANCOUVER

WATERFRONT

JAMES P. DELGADO

Vancouver Maritime Museum

Stanton Atkins & Dosil Publishers

CONTENTS

Chapter One   I   The Northwest Coast

Chapter Two   21   Skid Road Logging Port 1858–1886

Chapter Three   43   Rails Meet the Sea 1887–1913

Chapter Four   79   Dreams and Development 1914–1939

Chapter Five   107   The Boom Years 1940–1959

Chapter Six   137   Rise of the Ports 1960–to the present

180   Acknowledgements
       Sources
182   Index
185   Credits and permissions

THE NORTHWEST COAST

FORGED IN VOLCANIC FIRE and sculpted by successive glaciers, the rugged coast of British Columbia we see today was formed as the ice melted ten thousand years ago. Burrard Inlet is an artifact of those long-ago forces, the drowned course of a river that flowed through a narrow valley before the last ice age. At the First Narrows – the Lions Gate – the river plunged down a waterfall and spread out over a broad sandy plain on its way to the distant sea. The crushing force of nearly 1,500 metres of glacial ice buried this ancient landscape.

Ornately carved, this cedar and iron halibut hook with a braided cedar bark cord reflects the artistry and skill of both its carver and those who fished with it.

As the ice retreated, the land reappeared. Worn and shaped by the ice, the river valley became submerged as the ocean rose a hundred metres, flooding in through the lowlands and fed by melted glaciers, leaving the former riverbed an arm of the sea.

It was the sea that people followed to reach this land, recently emerged from the glacial freeze raw and new. The first humans landed on these shores in skin boats they had rowed and paddled out of the Sub-Arctic. These prehistoric mariners followed the coast, living off the abundant resources of an unpopulated land. Attracted by the thick forests of cedar and a seemingly endless supply of fish and molluscs, some of the ancient mariners stopped and settled here.

These first peoples discovered that when the tide fell, the table was set. The sea and its harvests sustained them, provided goods for trade and inspired the creation of small fishing canoes, large long-distance trading canoes and sleek racing craft. These were a people of the sea more than they were a people of the forest. Their homes, built facing the water, were in the transition zone from land to sea. The beaches were lined with canoes that provided the means for extended voyages of trade, plunder and war, as well as harvests from the ocean. These eager traders, fishermen and hunters built a series of settlements in the region some 8,000 years ago. By 3,000 years ago, they had settled the shores of modern-day Burrard Inlet, False Creek, English Bay and the Fraser River. These ancestors of the Musqueam, Squamish and Tseil-waututh peoples shared the area and

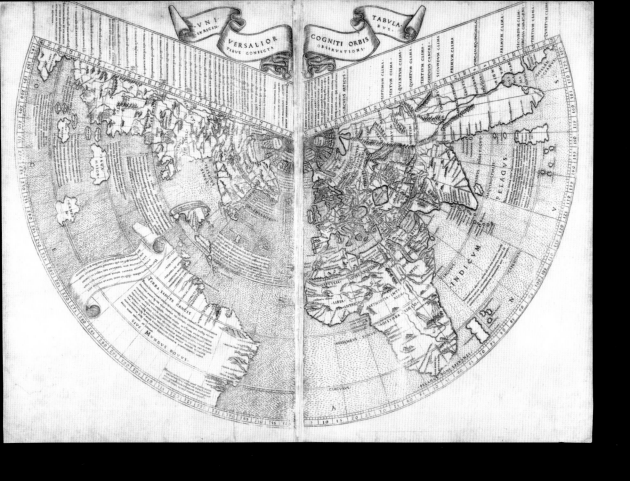

The first world map to show what is now Canada, this 1503 chart of the world by Claudius Ptolemy, represents the globe as Europeans knew it within the first decade of Columbus' voyages. What will become known as British Columbia – and indeed all the Pacific Ocean – is *terra* and *mare incognita*, or unknown lands and seas, except to the peoples who have inhabited those lands and traversed and worked on those waters for millennia.

THE COAST SALISH CANOE

The Salish canoe was the first watercraft to ply the waters of what we now call Vancouver Harbour, the Fraser River and the Gulf of Georgia, and, as versatile long-distance craft, to range up and down the coast into the territory of other peoples.

The canoes of the Coast Salish were artistic creations, a link to the spiritual world and essential craft for harvesting from the sea, and for travel, trade and war. As old as the culture that created it, the canoe is an ancient craft that has lasted into the 21st century without much change. Hewn out of the living form of a tree, usually red cedar, these canoes, at the time of the first European arrival, ranged in size from less than three metres to twenty-three metres in length.

Anthropologist Leslie Lincoln describes them as the products of master canoe builders. "Steam-bending of the log was used to increase the vessel's beam and create an outward-sloping sheer. Bow and stern pieces were ingeniously scarfed on the steambent hull" to create the "resulting fine lines of a gracefully rising bow, sloping sheer and protective stern" of the Coast Salish canoe.

After a decline and near extinction of the canoe in the face of the great cultural changes brought by the settlement of the coast by non-native peoples, the Salish canoe made a dramatic return in the late 20th century. Modern master canoe builders emerged, and a variety of canoes have taken to the water once more. In 2002, First Nations peoples from Alaska, British Columbia and Washington gathered with their canoes on the shores of Burrard Inlet as guests of the Squamish Nation. Races, feasts and a way of life regained through the return of the canoe were celebrated.

The Salish canoe, like the people who created it, has persisted and survived.

Salish canoe under sail in Coal Harbour, circa 1874, an adaptive blend of imported technology and traditional design.

its resources, intermarrying and trading. Products harvested from the ocean reached far inland in exchange for commodities from the interior, all part of a complex series of commercial relations that used both sea and river as an easier way to travel than overland through thick forests and steep mountains. Those same waterswould bring other peoples from far away, with dramatic consequences.

Asian seafarers may have reached the ocean coast of British Columbia long before any European explorers touched these shores. The kuroshio, or "black current," sweeps along the North Pacific from Japan to Vancouver Island, and for centuries seafaring junks and fishing craft from Japan crossed the ocean. Asian iron, predating the first known contact with Europeans in 1774, has emerged from archaeological sites, suggesting some form of interaction. Whether these visitors ever returned home is the subject of debate. Many of the craft that arrived on the Northwest Coast might have drifted, damaged by storms, across the open ocean, with dead or dying crews, or no crews at all. After 1639, when Japan sealed itself off to most foreigners, the government ordered shipbuilders to construct purposely weak craft to keep Japanese sailors close to home. According to Japanese records, more than 1,800 Japanese craft vanished between 1639 and the 1850s. Archaeologists believe that some ended up

The Fairfield Island mystery knife. Evidence of ancient Asian seafarers?

wrecked off Vancouver Island's shores.

Did any of these Asian seafarers reach the interior waters near present-day Vancouver? In 1932, pioneer Alexander McLean, who had first visited Burrard Inlet in 1858, reminisced about the past to Vancouver City archivist Major J.S. Matthews. Matthews wrote, "Mr. McLean made some remark about 'the Chinamen were here before the white man;' my note is incomplete – he spoke very fast, too fast to get it all down, and now he is dead." We may never know, but tantalizing traces suggest that even if the ships and their crews did not, then some of the goods they carried did. In 1925, a settler near Chilliwack, inland from the mouth of the Fraser, discovered a strange iron knife buried on the riverbank of Fairfield Island. Curved like a Malaysian kris, the mystery blade is thought by some to be an artifact of Asian origin. Now in the collections of the Vancouver Maritime Museum, the knife may be a reminder of early, ill-fated visitors from the other side of the Pacific.

The next visitors to these waters were European mariners seeking a legendary passage to the Far East. Ever since Christopher Columbus left Spain on what he thought would be a short voyage to the riches of Cathay, instead encountering the Americas, seamen had sought an easy ocean passage through the North American landmass. Known variously as the Straits of Anian or the Northwest Passage, this presumed aquatic shortcut inspired English, Spanish and Dutch mariners to scour the Atlantic and Pacific coasts in search of an entrance. That there was such a passage was certain, at least to the learned men of the day. English soldier and adventurer Sir Humphrey Gilbert argued that a Northwest Passage had to exist, based on travellers' accounts, ancient authorities and "physical evidence" that he had assembled. In 1576 Gilbert published a book, *A Discourse for a Discoverie for a New Pasage to Cathaia*, firing the popular imagination with his assertion that the passage was "the onely way for our princes, to possesse the wealthe of all the easte parts (as they terme them) of the world, which is infinite."

Gilbert's book inspired a voyage to the eastern shores of Canada and the fringes of the Arctic, under the command of privateer Martin Frobisher in 1576. A year later, another enterprising and avaricious English freebooter, Francis Drake, set out on a voyage that would take him around the world by way of the vast Pacific Ocean, then entirely under the control of England's rival, Spain. Drake's voyage, ostensibly to explore the Pacific and plunder Spanish shipping, may have had a secret purpose of seeking a western entrance to the Straits of Anian while Frobisher searched in the east. Whether Drake reached the sheltered waters of the Inside Passage between Vancouver Island and the mainland or the site of today's Vancouver is the subject of debate among scholars.

Walter J. Phillips
Howe Sound, 1935

Walter Phillips' woodcut evocatively captures the rugged, ice-carved landscape of the Greater Vancouver region.

These 19th century telescopes once guided mariners at sea and into Greater Vancouver's ports. The telescope in the middle is served with line—an art form that eventually transited from sea to shore.

many who doubted its veracity, mariners venturing to the Northwest Coast kept a weather eye peeled for the "Straits [sic] of Juan de Fuca."

Explorers Juan Perez, Francisco Bodega y Quadra and James Cook bypassed the Strait that now bears Juan de Fuca's name on their voyages of 1774, 1775, 1778 and 1779, staying offshore until well north. Cook was seeking the North West Passage and dismissed the "pretended Strait of Juan de Fuca" with the comment there was not "the least probability that ever such thing existed." Landing at Nootka, his men traded with the local people and in the process obtained hundreds of sea otter pelts. When those pelts sold at fantastic prices to eager Russian fur merchants, Cook's officers and men realized that the soft, luxuriant furs they had gathered through trade for what they had deemed mere trinkets were worth a fortune. While they never returned to capitalize on their discovery, published accounts of Cook's voyage spurred a rush by mariners and merchants to the North West Coast after 1784. It was one of them, Captain Charles Barkley, who finally spotted the modern Strait of Juan de Fuca and, realizing it might be the source of the two-century-old tale, named it.

While the threat of Russian interest in the region and its furs led to the Spanish establishment of a fortified settlement at Nootka in 1789, it was the burgeoning maritime fur trade and the influx of British

Spanish mariners did probe the Pacific coast in the 16th and 17th centuries, although an official policy of secrecy means that their comings and goings are still shrouded in mystery. One voyage that has a ring of plausibility was a 1592 expedition from Mexico, piloted by Greek seaman Apostolos Valerianos, who was in the employ of the Spanish crown under the name "Juan de Fuca." Decades after the voyage, Valerianos, then in Venice, confided to English traveller Michael Lok that they had sailed north, past a prominent rock pillar and into a "broad Inlet of Sea, betweene 47, and 48, degrees of Latitude," and for twenty days pushed up an inland waterway to find a land rich in gold, silver and other precious items. Lok published Valerianos' tale in 1625, and although there were

The Arnold 176 Chronometer

Chronometers keep accurate time at sea and help navigators plot latitude. During Captain George Vancouver's "Voyage of Discovery," between 1791–1795, Vancouver's officers used this chronometer as they surveyed and charted the Pacific Coast of North America.

John Arnold of London manufactured No. 176 in 1787. Captain Matthew Flinders, the first mariner to chart the entire coast of Australia, later used Arnold 176. After Flinders' voyage (1801–1803), Captain William Bligh used the chronometer in 1806 when he served as Governor of New South Wales in Australia.

Captain George Vancouver and his crews "manned the oars and mapped the coast" of British Columbia between 1792 and 1795 in the Royal Navy vessels *Discovery* and *Chatham*. Highly accurate, they opened the region to further European (and American) incursions and ultimately settlement. This chart, "Shewing Part of the Coast of N.W. America" was prepared for publication by Lieut. Joseph Baker and published in Vancouver's posthumous *A Voyage of Discovery....Round the World*.

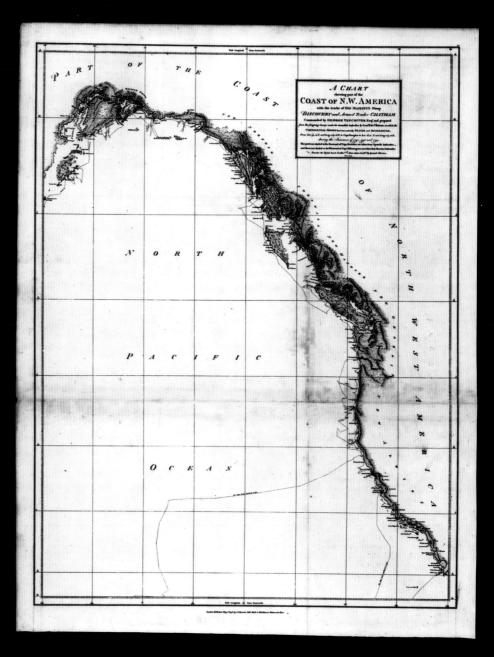

PETER PUGET'S ACCOUNT OF THE SQUAMISH

We contrived by Signs to convince each other of reciprocal Friendship. May we not from the Circumstances of the Musquet [musket] infer, that their tribe heretofore were unacquainted with Europeans, else why betray so much Astonishment – Although Indians familiarized to Fire Arms in general shrink from the Report as if to avoid the Effect. The Ideas of these People could only be understood from the Expression of Countenance & evident Signs of Fear – I therefore have no Doubt but we are the first Europeans who have penetrated thus far into the Streights, though it has been alleged that the Copper Ornaments in general Use with most of the Tribes we have met must have been procured from Visitors.

and American traders that had the greatest impact. When Spanish authorities arrested British fur traders and seized their ships as they staked their claim to Nootka, Britain and Spain nearly went to war. Diplomatic exchanges over the next few years settled the issue in Britain's favour, but both governments sent expeditions to the coast to chart its shores and seek the elusive passage. In 1791, and again in 1792, Spanish and British explorers sailed into the Strait of Juan de Fuca to reach the waters that would one day become Vancouver harbour.

Spanish explorer José Maria Narváez reconnoitered the entrance to the harbour in the schooner *Santa Saturnina* in the summer of 1791, but this first recorded European visitor did not proceed into the protected inner harbour, cruising only into today's English Bay. Nonetheless, Narváez did "discover," for Europeans, the inlet where one day the great port would rise. His chart outlines a sketchy shore and features that he named the Boca de Florida Blanca (now Burrard Inlet), the Islas de Langara (Point Grey), Punta de la Bodega (Point Ferguson) and the Bocas del Carmelo (Howe Sound). In 1792, Narváez's track was followed by Britain's George Vancouver, and a simultaneous Spanish expedition commanded by Dionisio Alcalá Galiano and Cayetano Valdés.

Vancouver, with his two ships, *Discovery* and *Chatham*, the latter commanded by Lt. William Broughton, was the first to sail into what they named "Burrard's Canal." On June 13 Vancouver's ships passed the Squamish settlement of Wh'mullutsthun as they entered the inlet, and about fifty people followed *Discovery* and *Chatham* for a while, offering a gift of fish "with the greatest decorum and civility," as Vancouver commented. He also noted that "these good people, finding we were inclined to make some return for their hospitality, shewed [sic] much understanding in preferring iron to copper." After anchoring for the night off the entrance to Indian Arm, Vancouver departed the next morning, heading up the coast into Howe Sound and Jervis Inlet.

On June 27, passing English Bay en route to his ships, anchored farther south,

Vancouver met up with the schooners *Sutil* and *Mexicana*, commanded by Galiano and Valdés. The British and Spanish explorers, each aware of the other's presence in this "far side of the world," had encountered each other previously. But now, at what would become a historic meeting, they found that they were, in a sense, duplicating each other's work. Perhaps, in the best tradition of the enlightened age in which they lived they should collaborate – for the sake of science and discovery? Within a few days, Vancouver returned in *Discovery* and *Chatham*, and the four vessels, joining forces for further exploration, headed north, leaving the waters and shores of what would be Greater Vancouver behind.

Before they departed, the Spaniards charted Indian Arm, but neither group entered or charted the Fraser River. Lt. Peter Puget, writing in his journal, noted, "the land abreast to the Eastward is low & about 3 leagues distant. Two places in that direction held much the appearance of large Rivers, but the Shoals hitherto have prevented our having any Communication with them."

The lucrative maritime fur trade on the coast brought increasing numbers of British and American ships to the British Columbia coast, including traders who sailed their ships into the Strait of Juan de Fuca in search of furs. Fierce competition and heavy demand for fur had two results:

HOW THE SQUAMISH REMEMBER GEORGE VANCOUVER

As told by Squamish historian Louis Miranda and Chief Philip Joe: Early one morning in the month called Tim-kwis-ᴋᴡᴀs ('hot time'), an old man living near the mouth of the Squamish River had gone down to wash. As he raised his head, he saw an "island" where no island had been before. The old man was alarmed and ran back to his house to wake his relatives. "There is an island in the sound – a floating island," he told them. The old man knew it was an island for it was covered with skeletons of trees thrust skyward . . . . It was decided that the men would go out in their canoes to see the island. As they grew near, they saw it wasn't a floating island at all, but a very large canoe, a strange canoe. Soon, men appeared and walked around the canoe. But what strange men they were! Every part of their body was covered except for their faces, which were white. My people scrutinized them. Finally, some of the elders came up with an explanation: these people are from the land of the dead. And they are wrapped in their burial blankets!

One of the dead people stepped forward. He had smoke coming from his mouth and it appeared that he was eating fire. The man motioned for my ancestors to go on board . . . . The Squamish looked around the strange, large canoe and when it was time to leave . . . the white people lowered into the canoes some presents, including a barrel and a few boxes . . . . The story passed down by my ancestors tells how Vancouver provided gifts of pilot biscuits, whisky and white flour – unfamiliar foods that they used with results that were initially comical . . . . Apparently Vancouver then sailed north, for his travels up the coast can be traced by the elders' stories of mysterious floating islands that appeared offshore, and then, just as quickly as they arrived, sailed beyond the next point.

Plano
del Estrecho de Juan de Fuca Reconocido desde
los 48° meridiano 1790 por Dn Manuel Quimper en
el de 1791 Dn Manuel Eliza por orn del Sr Dn...
...

Longitud occidental del Puerto de S. Blas

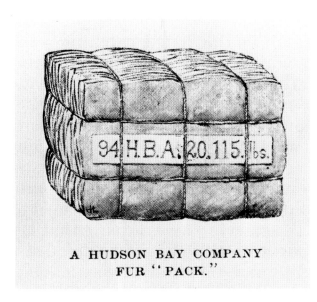

A HUDSON BAY COMPANY FUR "PACK."

At Fort Vancouver, Fort Langley and other outposts, Hudson's Bay traders cleaned, sorted and packaged furs into large bales for shipment by sea back to England.

the practical extinction of the sea otter on the coast and the triumph of the American "Boston tillikums" (as they were called in the regional Chinook jargon) in the trade. The Americans were shrewd bargainers, and when trade failed they resorted to violence to gain what they wanted. To feed the need for fur, peoples in the interior gathered furs and sent them to powerful coastal chiefs who controlled the flow of trade with the foreigners on their shores. British efforts to win back the trade, and to secure control of a coast it felt was Britain's by right of discovery and diplomatic negotiation with Spain and Russia, led to the arrival of the Hudson's Bay Company (HBC), in the early 19th century.

Established in 1670 on the shores of the great bay that gave the company its name,

the HBC spanned the continent by 1821, when a merger with its bitter rival, the North West Company, added that Montreal-based firm's Pacific coast assets to the HBC. The Company soon established its own Pacific base at Fort Vancouver, roughly 160 kilometres up the Columbia River, and set about taking control of the coast and its trade. Through the acquisition and construction of a fleet of coastal trading vessels, it built up a private navy, which augmented a series of forts the Company established on the coast. In the summer of 1825, the HBC supply brig *William and Ann* made a voyage up the Inside Passage to trade for furs and reconnoitre the region. The brig's master, Henry Hanwell, made a brief survey of the mouth of the Fraser River but did not enter it.

In June 1827, the Company's 70-ton schooner *Cadboro*, under the command of Aemilius Simpson, finally entered and charted the Fraser. The HBC had ordered Dr. John McLoughlin, in charge of its Pacific-based Columbia Department, to establish an outpost at the entrance to the river. *Cadboro*, with the supplies, equipment and men for the new post, surveyed the river as Simpson made his way forty-five kilometres up it before finding a suitable site. That outpost, which they named Fort Langley, would prosper, and although its principal commodity for shipment was fur, its secondary commodity proved to be the abundant salmon of the Fraser. The

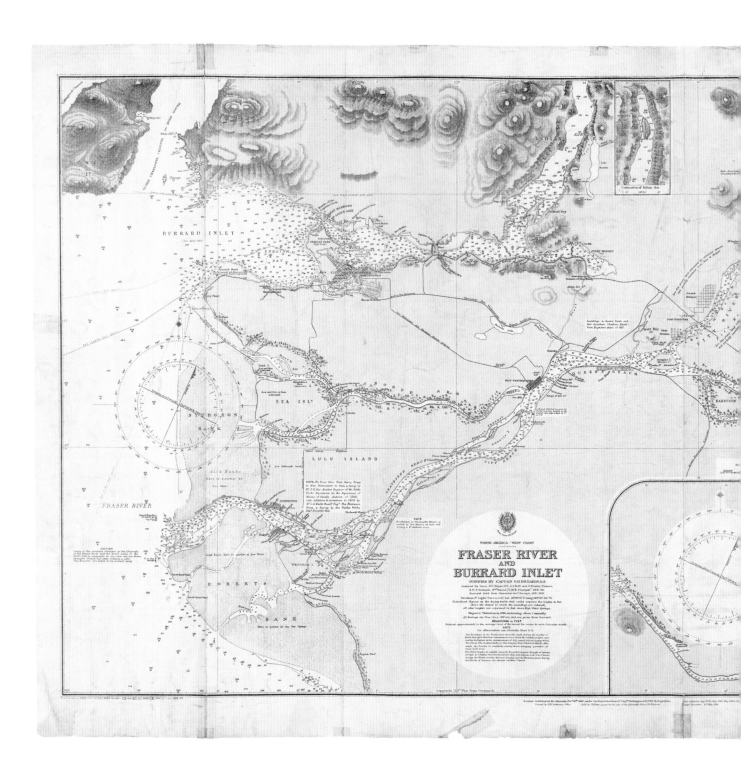

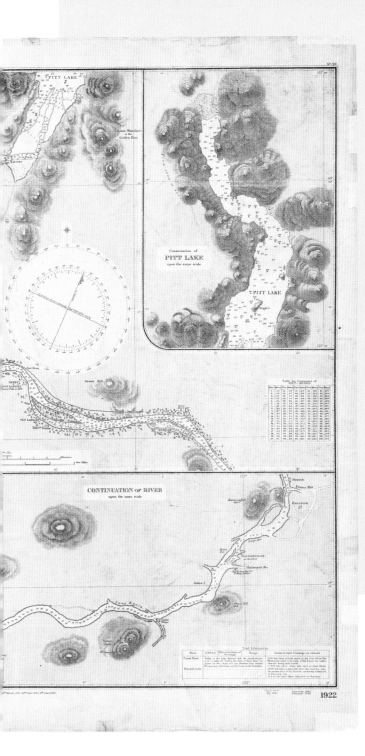

POSSESSION BY NAME

Even though other people had lived in the region for thousands of years, both the Spanish and British explorers who came to the British Columbia coast in 1791–1795 "took formal possession" of the lands and waters in the names of their sovereigns. Part of the process of taking possession was the charting and mapping of the region, and establishing place names. Many of the names of today's prominent landmarks were bestowed by these early European mariners. The Spanish were responsible for the San Juan, Texada and Lasqueti islands, for example. George Vancouver named Point Grey, Point Atkinson, Burrard Inlet, False Creek, Howe Sound, Puget Sound, Mount Baker and Mount Rainier – just some of the 388 place names he bestowed during his "voyage of discovery." Many of the names are those of Vancouver's patrons, friends and crew.

The competing interests of Spain and Britain meant that each expedition placed its own names on landmarks or bodies of water. The Spanish names have for the most part been swept aside in favour of the British ones since Britain's claim was ultimately the successful one. The Canal del Nuestra Señora del Rosario, for example, is today known by the name George Vancouver gave it, the Gulf of Georgia.

Ignored for the most part were the names the original inhabitants had given to the land and water. Pookcha (floating whale's back), known to most Vancouverites as Spanish Banks, Sun-ahk (inside, at the head) or Kitsilano Point and Stalo (river) or the Fraser, are but a few of the names that had lasted for thousands of years, and persist today for the Musqueam, Squamish and Tseil-waututh peoples. Some original words and names do persist in anglicized form: Capilano, Chilliwack, Coquitlam, Kitsilano, Kwantlen and Tsawwassen are among them.

The first detailed chart of Burrard Inlet and the Fraser River, based on the initial survey by Captain George Henry Richards and his crew, published in 1860 and revised in 1891.

first years were lean; by 1830, Fort Langley had only prepared 300 barrels of salmon for export. But the harvests and shipments grew through the 1840s and '50s, a harbinger of the region's future fishing industry.

The HBC built a new fort at the southern tip of Vancouver Island in 1843. Situated on the banks of the small natural harbour the local natives called Camosun, Fort Victoria became the Company's Pacific headquarters in 1849, replacing Fort Vancouver. The fur trade was in decline by then, and the HBC eagerly sought new commodities for trade. The California Gold Rush introduced a new market for provisions grown at HBC farms and orchards, fish from the Fraser and manufactured goods from England imported by the Company for the fur trade, but it was two abundant natural resources that attracted the most attention. The first was lumber. In October 1849, the barque *Collooney* shipped 42,270 board feet of British Columbia lumber to San Francisco, the beginning of a trade and an industry that would dominate the coast and the ports that would arise on it. One of the ports born out of the lumber trade would be the future City of Vancouver.

The second commodity was coal. Coal beds on the northern end of Vancouver Island were mined with limited success through 1851, but it was the discovery of new coal beds near today's Nanaimo that would ultimately prove plentiful. In early 1851, as the HBC continued to seek new lands to till, log and mine, Chief Factor James Douglas sent a small scouting party out from Fort Langley "for the purpose of examining the Country between Fraser River and Burrard's Canal, which we have just heard contains extensive plains – The party will also examine the Coal on Fraser's River, and other beds of Coal reported by Indians in Burrard's Canal."

In March, Douglas reported that the expedition had made "no discovery of much present importance." "Thin surface patches" of coal had been found, including one "at the entrance of Burrard's Canal" (today's Coal Harbour), but it was not worth pursuing. However, the lands between the river and inlet, today's Vancouver, were "generally level and thickly wooded, principally with a magnificent growth of pines...[with] a number of small streams capable of driving machinery [for sawmills], which may be converted to good account as the settlement of the country advances." That settlement would come, but only in response to British Columbia's own discovery of gold and the rush that followed in 1858. Only subsequently would settlers and entrepreneurs take advantage of the rich timber resources and a magnificent natural harbour that allowed easy access to the mills that would spring up after that year.

Joseph Baker's Signals Book from the Vancouver voyage. In the days of sail, and the early Royal Navy, young officers learned their trade at sea. One of the tasks was hand illustrating and writing a "book of signals" as a guide to the various flags and signals ships used to communicate with each other.

Joseph Baker (1768–1817) joined the Royal Navy at the age of thirteen. He served with Captain George Vancouver as third, later second and finally as first Lieutenant on board HMS *Discovery*. Vancouver prized Baker highly, and named Mt. Baker in Washington State for him during the voyage. Baker was the first on the expedition to sight the mountain that would bear his name.

Following the voyage, Baker continued his career, gaining promotion to Commander in 1799 and Captain in 1802. His career included naval actions against Denmark in the Napoleonic Wars, but in August 1811, his ship, HMS *Tartar*, stranded on a sandbar and wrecked. Everyone was saved, but the incident ended Baker's career afloat. He commanded a prisoner of war camp ashore, and then retired.

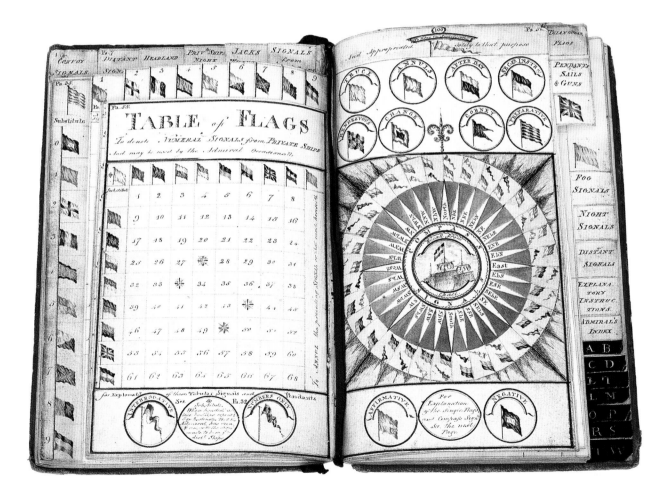

Chapter Two

SKID ROAD LOGGING PORT

1858–1886   BRITISH AUTHORITY over the Northwest Coast, challenged by the United States' Pacific interests, achieved a measure of security in 1846 when the two nations signed a treaty establishing the international boundary at the 49th Parallel. Britain's maritime interests and possesion of Vancouver Island were protected by the boundary's dip down the Gulf of Georgia and halfway across the Strait of Juan de Fuca. That meant that the ships of both nations could stay in their own territorial waters, whether bound north to Fort Victoria or south to American-owned Puget Sound. Boundary notwithstanding, the Strait and the Inside Passage would soon become a busy thoroughfare for the ships of both nations.

From the early 1850s, ships calling for lumber on Vancouver Island, HBC trading vessels and British warships frequented these waters. Regular arrivals by sailing ships and steamers between San Francisco, an important market, and Victoria, now the capital of the new Crown Colony of Vancouver Island, kept the lines of communication and commerce open.

News of gold discoveries in the Queen Charlotte Islands in 1851 had sparked a small exodus of American gold seekers by ship to the area, but little in the way of returns, and the ferocity of the Haida, who seized and burned the American ship *Susan Sturgis* in 1852, temporarily dampened Yankee interest in northern gold mines.

Gold discoveries on the banks of the Fraser River in late 1857 sparked a new rush. When the HBC steamer *Otter* arrived at San Francisco in February 1858 with 800 ounces (22.5 kg) of gold from the Fraser, the news spread like wildfire. *Commodore*, a veteran coaster, had first steamed to the Pacific to carry gold seekers to California several years earlier. Now she headed north to Victoria, overcrowded with would-be miners and speculators. The influx of Californians by sea was incredible; by the summer of 1858 some 18,000 Americans had arrived in Victoria, overwhelming the town's British and native population, and many had headed across the Strait of Georgia and up the Fraser to reach the

The Hudson's Bay Company's coastal steamer *Otter*, the Company's second steam-powered vessel on the coast. *Otter* arrived in 1853 to assist the steamer *Beaver* in the fur trade.

"diggings" at Hill's Bar. The Hudson's Bay Company capitalized on the rush by refitting its steamship *Beaver* as a passenger-carrying riverboat. *Beaver*'s regular runs up the Fraser ended in May 1860 when American entrepreneurs introduced their own riverboats to the Fraser and paid the HBC a thousand dollars a month to keep *Beaver* out of service.

With the Fraser now the route to the gold regions, the British government passed an act to make the mainland a new Crown Colony in 1858. James Douglas of the HBC, now the new Colony's governor, journeyed up the Fraser on board *Beaver* to Fort Langley, where he formally proclaimed the creation of "British Columbia"

on November 19th. The following year, New Westminster, a new river port and capital for the Colony, was established on the banks of the Fraser. The river, with its sandbars and freeze-ups, made New Westminster a problematic capital. The new Colony needed a major port close to New Westminster to ensure that regular communication by sea was possible. Colonel Richard Moody of the Royal Engineers had his men cut trails through the wilderness to the protected harbour on Burrard Inlet in 1859 and 1860, where he laid out a series of government reserves. In the event of trouble, Royal Navy ships at Burrard Inlet could send marines overland to New Westminster over Moody's trails, one of

This busy scene, shown in this front page illustration of Fort Langley from *Harper's Weekly* of October 9, 1858, demonstrates how the bustling trading activity involving native and settler watercraft near the HBC fort caught the imagination of readers as far away as New York City.

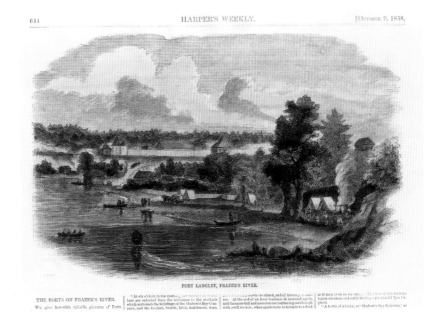

which is today's Kingsway.

As Moody worked ashore, Royal Navy surveyor Captain George Henry Richards, aboard HMS *Plumper*, exhaustively surveyed Burrard Inlet, English Bay and False Creek in 1859. Richards' work recognized the potential of the future port, but for commerce and not for the Royal Navy, which ultimately decided to base its ships in the Pacific closer to the open ocean at Esquimalt near Victoria.

What ultimately attracted interest in Burrard Inlet as an anchorage were the dense stands of trees that lined the inlet's shores. In the winter of 1862–63, New Westminster architect and builder Thomas Wilson Graham erected a sawmill on the north shore of the inlet, which he advertised in the New Westminster *British Columbian* of July 1, 1863:

> Pioneer Mills, Burrard Inlet. The subscribers having completed their sawmill on the above inlet, five miles above the first narrows, are now prepared to furnish Fir, Cedar, Spruce Lumber, also tongued and Grooved flooring to be delivered at the mill, New Westminster, or Victoria, Vancouver Island, at prices lower than Puget Sound lumber, T.W. Graham & Co.

Graham's aptly named Pioneer Mills had few European neighbours. Across the inlet, young Englishman John Morton had constructed a small cabin and was digging for coal and clay to make bricks for export. Morton's business never took off, and the hopes for a coal mine equal to those at Nanaimo ended in 1866, when a deep shaft cut into the bedrock of the shores of Coal Harbour confirmed the Hudson's Bay Company's 1851 assessment that what lay there were "thin surface patches." The fortunes to be made on Burrard Inlet would not be from coal, nor would the inlet profit from the ongoing gold mining in the interior. However, thanks to the deepwater port's access to a world market for lumber, the inlet's timber was as good as gold to its early settlers.

The Pioneer Mills sold lumber to New Westminster, Nanaimo and Victoria, beginning in August 1863 with a shipment of 25,000 feet (7500 metres) of three-inch (7.5-centimetre) planks for the New Westminster levee carried out of the inlet, around Point Grey and up the Fraser aboard a barge towed by the steamer *Flying Dutchman*. Graham's mill did not prosper – "the competition of the mills in New Westminster, the isolated situation, and the difficulties, delays and expense of transport were too much and too many for the little Pioneer Mills," according to historian F.W. Howay – and in December it was sold at auction, passing to John Oscar Smith, a New Westminster grocer. Smith ran it as the "Burrard Inlet Mills" for a year. Under his tenure, the inlet made its first foreign shipment – 277,500 feet (83 250 metres) of lumber and

BEAVER

Built just outside London in 1835 for the Hudson's Bay Company, *Beaver* sailed to the Pacific coast in 1836. Arriving at the HBC's Fort Vancouver, on the banks of the Columbia River, *Beaver* was the first steamship to reach the North Pacific. The staunch little steamer ended up serving on the coast for another fifty-two years.

After working as a floating fur trading depot, and occasionally acting as a de facto naval vessel for the HBC's private fleet on the coast, *Beaver* retired from service in 1860 after a short tenure as a Fraser River gold rush passenger boat. Commissioned into the Royal Navy in 1862 under the command of Lt. Daniel Pender, the veteran steamship spent the next decade surveying BC's coastal inlets and islands. More than 200 place names were added to the coast, along with a thousand nautical miles of new charts. Like the explorers of the 18th century, Pender put the names of himself, his officers, patrons, friends and even the steamer's sky terrier mascot "Innis" on coastal landmarks.

Laid up again in 1872, *Beaver* languished until 1874, when the HBC sold her to locals who converted her into a tugboat. Working on the Strait of Juan de Fuca and in and out of Burrard Inlet, *Beaver* supplied logging camps and towed ships into Nanaimo for

"BEAVER"

The Pioneer Steamer, now lying on the rocks in the Narrows, Burrard Inlet, B.C., the first to ply on the Pacific waters. Sailed from the Thames and rounded the Horn in 1835.

The steamer *Beaver* as a Burrard Inlet tug and supply boat in March 1888. This is the last photograph taken of the historic steamer before it wrecked. Captain George Marchant stands at the wheelhouse door. The photograph is framed with wood and rigging taken from the stranded hulk.

coal and the inlet for lumber, and then pulled them out into the Strait from 1874 to 1888. The end finally came on July 26, 1888. Leaving Vancouver after a stint in a bar, the crew piled the old steamship on to the rocks of Prospect Point.

The assistant engineer, W.H. Evans, later recalled that they were hugging the shore when the steamer hit, "and that settled it." Caught at high tide, *Beaver* would not budge as the tide fell. "We all got off into the water," said Evans, "and waded ashore, walked through the park to the Sunnyside Hotel, and were at rest and peace . . . we had not long before we left the bartender with goodbyes, and promised we would see him again, but he did not expect to see us that quick."

Stuck on the rocks, *Beaver* remained a prominent Stanley Park landmark for the next four years. Souvenir hunters, well aware that the wreck was an historic ship, stripped the hulk of loose items before turning to the wood and metal with axes, crowbars and saws. In 1892, the wake from the passing side-wheeler *Yosemite* swept the rotting hull off the rocks and *Beaver* broke apart and sank.

Much of the wreck lies off Prospect Point despite the best efforts of souvenir hunters and collectors. The wreck is now a protected heritage site and is regularly dived and mapped by the Underwater Archaeological Society of British Columbia. Swept by fast tides, it is not an easy dive.

Walking sticks, some with silver mounts, made of wood salvaged from the wreck of *Beaver*.

Charles McCain of Vancouver salvaged some of the ship's copper and brass fittings from the hull and engines, and cast a series of medallions to accompany a history of the vessel he had written. These coins, fashioned into gilded cufflinks, with a descriptive card, were made and sold by McCain in the late 1890s.

A scratch-built "sailor's model," handmade and homespun, of *Beaver* at the end of her working life.

Sewell P. Moody's mill at Moodyville, 1872. In the foreground,
freshly cut logs float in the inlet,
awaiting milling. Wooden-hulled
sailing ships line the docks to
load; broadside (in profile) to the
dock, a ship is loading by the stern,
with long timbers slid into hatches
at the aft end of the hull.

Logging the virgin forests of Burrard Inlet. With a "steam donkey" behind them, loggers pose triumphantly beside a giant of the forest they have just felled.

16,000 pickets – tediously loaded aboard the barque *Ellen Lewis* between September 16 and November 9. Clearing New Westminster because the inlet was not a legal port of entry, *Ellen Lewis* sailed for Adelaide, Australia. Unfortunately for Smith, his lenders foreclosed his mortgage and sold the mill and 480 acres (192 hectares) of timber at auction.

The buyer this time was American Sewell P. "Sue" Moody, who improved the facilities, renamed it "The Burrard Inlet Lumber Mills," and put it back in operation in February 1865 with capital from two British Columbia partners and his San Francisco agent. Moody literally put the inlet on the map. Focusing on the international market, Moody quickly loaded a cargo aboard the barque *Glimpse* bound for

Sydney, Australia, shipped another load in the ship *Envoy* to Adelaide, and a third cargo for Mexico in the ship *Metropolis* within the space of three months. Moody's energy and drive were apparent. An 1868 account commented that "Moody has two mills, a steam and water mill, capable of cutting 80,000 feet [24 000 metres] per 24 hours; when necessary they work night and day. Stevedores can be employed at the mills for $5.00 per day. Pilotage $7.00 per foot; pilots can be had at Victoria or English Bay. Ballast can be thrown out in the inlet. No wharfage dues to pay."

Moody's business at what became known as Moodyville slowly but steadily increased as word spread of Burrard Inlet's superior lumber and the easy access of the port. His fourth customer was the barque *Kent*, which arrived to load lumber for Mexico. American competitors on Puget Sound and in San Francisco disparaged the inlet's products and the safety of the harbour, but Moody counterattacked, enlisting ship's masters who called to advertise in his favour. Captain S. MacLean of the barque *Barzillai*, after loading 400,000 feet of lumber for Callao, Peru, wrote to Messrs. Friedlander and Co. of San Francisco in November 1867 to report that: "My passage occupied seven days to Fuca Straits and seven to Burrard's Inlet. I stopped nowhere and did not employ a steam tug or pilot. My cargo consists of 400,000 feet. The harbour is safe and inexpensive."

Moody made sure Captain MacLean's letter was published, as was another from Captain William J. Looe of the ship *Chelsea*, who praised Moody's less expensive operation – and one free of the usual temptations for sailors: "Having loaded last year at Puget Sound, I find that my expenses do not amount to one-third of what they were there. The crews here are free from the temptation of a grog shop, and no idlers are allowed about this place."

Moody gained closer competition than Puget Sound in early 1865 when an irascible Englishman, Captain Edward Stamp, who had previously opened and closed mills elsewhere on the coast, erected a mill for a group of London-based partners. Stamp built their mill on the south shore of the inlet, at the site of today's Vancouver on the shores now occupied by Centerm. Stamp's Mill, as it was soon known, did not have all of its machinery in place to begin milling in 1865. Delays in receiving meant that two years would pass before Stamp went into production. But that did not mean he was idle. The "spar" side of the business went into full production, logging timber suitable for shaping into masts and yards for sailing ships.

Assisting Stamp was Jeremiah "Jerry" Rogers, a New Brunswick logger who set up camp on the southern shores of English Bay and began felling trees. Roger's camp, named Jericho (perhaps a play on "Jerry's Cove"), provided Stamp with the timber he needed to ship, commencing in August 1865 when the British ship *Aquila* loaded 251 spars cut by Rogers and then proceeded to Moody's mill for 138,705 feet (41 612 metres) of lumber before heading to Cork, Ireland.

A pattern of work developed over the next several years. Loggers like Rogers worked to cut down the massive forests that covered the site of today's Vancouver and Burnaby, starting at the water's edge and working inland. As the logging continued deeper into the forest, workers laid down log thoroughfares known as "skid roads" to slide their cuts to the mills at the water's edge. To ease the passage of the logs, workers turned to a product of the sea – the oil of the local dogfish – which was rendered and poured on to "grease the skids." Logs rolled down to the sea, where they were rafted and towed to Stamp's and Moody's mills. There the best, "some magnificent logs" of 180 feet (54 metres) or more, were saved to become spars, while the rest were cut and stacked on wharves to be cured and ready for loading when ships arrived.

In 1865, Moody had loaded four ships, in 1866 he loaded five, and in 1867 he loaded seven. In September 1867, with Stamp's Mill in full production, the inlet gained the distinction of having four vessels in port at the same time, a new record. That year was a hallmark; a "turning of the tide," for what followed was even more rapid growth of the mills' output and the rise of the skid

Taking a rest on the skid road. An ox team's crew pauses as they slide freshly cut logs down a "skid road" to the waters of English Bay.

The earliest roads were these log-paved paths to shore. Greased with fish oil, they facilitated clearing the forests.

S.P. MOODY

Sewell Prescott "Sue" Moody, a native of Maine, immigrated to British Columbia around 1859, and by 1861 had settled in New Westminster. In 1862, Moody made a small fortune by selling cattle he drove up from Oregon. Moody, with business partners James Van Bramer and Moses Ireland, started a sawmill on the Fraser, which unfortunately failed. In 1865 Moody purchased the bankrupt Burrard Inlet Mills. Under Moody, the mill slowly and then more rapidly prospered, expanding in the 1860s and surviving a disastrous fire that destroyed half of the mill.

In 1869, Moody married Janet Watson of Victoria and started a family. His mill continued to prosper, with the "enterprising Mr. Moody" driving the business. The Moody family and the business were both dealt a terrible blow in early November 1875. Steaming out of Victoria to San Francisco on a business trip aboard the steamer *Pacific*, Moody died when the steamer rammed the passing barque *Orpheus* in the night and quickly filled with water when the rotten timbers in her aged bow gave way. Only two out of 277 aboard survived, one of them, the ship's quartermaster, after drifting for seventy-six hours on the open ocean.

Wreckage from the lost steamer and a few bodies drifted ashore off Neah Bay and on Vancouver Island, some of them carried by the tide back to Victoria. Six weeks after the wreck, a "gentleman walking along Beacon Hill beach" picked up a small fragment of wood, whitewashed and inscribed with a simple penciled message from beyond the grave – "S.P. Moody – All Lost." Moody's last message outlived his mill, which closed in 1901. After ninety-six years in the hands of the Moody family, the message was donated to the Vancouver Maritime Museum, where it remains on prominent display.

A poignant message from beyond the grave, this fragment of wood from the ill-fated *Pacific* bears S.P. Moody's signature and the note "all lost."

road port. Between January 1867 and June 1868, Moody loaded 33 ships with 8,300 tons – nearly six million board feet – of lumber. In 1868, Moody built a second mill and a large wharf capable of loading a dozen ships to meet the demand, claiming he could now produce 100,000 feet of lumber a day to load into the waiting ships that called to take Burrard Inlet timber to China, South America, Australia, Great Britain, and the United States, where the port of San Francisco took the bulk of the inlet's exports.

On the south shore, two new settlements had arisen. Brighton, near the Second Narrows, and "Gastown" near Stamp's Mill, precipitated by Yorkshire

The waterfront at the Granville town site in 1885. This tiny settlement will soon become Vancouver. The little steamboat in the stream, near the narrow floating dock, is the ferry and mail carrier *Leonora*, the pioneer vessel of the Union Steam Ship Company of British Columbia.

mariner and trader Captain John Deighton, were small shoreside towns at the water's edge with no more than ten buildings between the two of them. Deighton, known as "Gassy Jack," landed with a whisky barrel and used its contents to secure the labour of a group of bystanders to build the saloon that was Gastown's genesis, much to the chagrin of mill officials who now had to contend with drunken loggers and sailors. The settlement of Brighton became the more sedate company town of Hastings Mill, a match for Moodyville, S.P. Moody's company town that had grown up around his two mills on the North Shore.

The infant port gained its first towboat in July 1866 when Captain Stamp commissioned the construction of the 146-foot (44-metre) sidewheel steamer *Isabel* in Victoria. Carrying passengers and towing log rafts and barges, *Isabel* towed ships into and out of the inlet and brought people and supplies to Stamp's Mill. Ferry service across the inlet began in 1865 when Englishman "Navvy" Jack Thomas began rowing people from Brighton to Moodyville.

In 1867, the small steam ferry *Sea Foam*, owned by Captain James Van Bramer, Moody's business partner, commenced service, connecting Brighton, Moodyville and Stamp's Mill. Other improvements included the establishment of pilot service, with the pilots building a small station at Pilot's Cove (near today's Caulfeild in West Vancouver) and, in 1875, the construction

Old Prospect Point
Vancouver B.C. #17

John Blomfield
Old Prospect Point, circa 1910

Another view of Prospect Point,
showing a salmon fishing boat
pausing while working the waters
of the inlet.

Squatter's shacks on the shores of Coal Harbour on Deadman's Island. Originally a burial site for the Squamish and later for plague victims, the island was illegally settled after Vancouver was founded.

1877, with the news that a transcontinental railroad was to be built across Canada, speculators began to buy up property on the assumption that the skid road port might become something bigger.

But the promise of a future metropolis and major port was still a dream in the mid-1870s. Burrard Inlet was now crowded with ships, and the settlements were growing with new arrivlas, many of them sailors who left their ships to start a new life ashore. The result was a diverse collection of nationalities and races on the inlet. In addition to some 800 Musqueam, Squamish and Tseil-waututh, about 800 non-natives lived on the inlet – including Portuguese, Chilean, Hawaiian, Russian, Finnish, Austrian, German, Dutch, Spanish, French, Belgian, Swedish, American, English, Irish and Scottish mill workers, Chinese, and Philip and Josephine Sullivan, American free blacks who had left California for British Columbia during the Fraser River gold rush, and who now operated one of Granville's restaurants. All port cities are a polyglot, and modern-day Vancouver's cosmopolitan outlook and celebrated cultural diversity was born of its humble origins as a bustling lumber port.

Outside of the inlet, on the Fraser, New Westminster – no longer the capital once an amalgamated Vancouver Island and British Columbia had joined together as a new colony and selected Victoria as the seat of government in 1868 – continued as

of the area's first lighthouse at Point Atkinson.

No longer interested in competing with Burrard Inlet's mills, California merchants and entrepreneurs had begun to invest in more ships and in the expansion of both Moody and Stamp's mills. In 1870, following Stamp's retirement and a lawsuit between him and his former employers, the mill was sold at auction and bought by San Francisco investors who operated it as "Hastings Mill." That same year, a government surveyor laid out a new town site around Gassy Jack's saloon. That town site, subdivided and offered for sale by the government as "Granville," was the genesis of the modern city of Vancouver. Its sole business was to provide goods and services to the loggers, sailors and mill hands, but by

Spratt's "Ark" or Oilery on the shores of Burrard Inlet in 1884. The site is today occupied by the Marine Building on Burrard Street.

ted tons of fish out of the river, a series of canneries harvested the take. In 1878, eight canneries on the Fraser, including Deas', produced over five million one-pound (454-gram) cans of salmon. By 1882 the numbers had nearly doubled.

Back on Burrard Inlet, Captain Joseph Spratt had built British Columbia's first floating cannery and Burrard Inlet's first industrial facility when he moored the self-propelled barge *Spratt's Ark* off Granville's shores in 1883. Built at William Allen's shipyard in Victoria in 1883 for Joseph Spratt, the *Ark* was a squarely built floating fish reduction plant and cannery that Spratt moored just west of the foot of Burrard Street. Every old-timer in town knew the *Ark's* whereabouts. They couldn't help missing it because of the stench that came out of the floating plant. Also known as "Spratt's Oilery," the plant took tons of herring and extracted the oil from them. According to one pioneer, J.H. Rowlings, "The herrings used to be very numerous; thick in the water. We used to get a pole and drive a lot of nails in so that the sharp ends stuck out like spikes. . . . The pole would be, say, twenty feet long, with the nails clustered at one end, then you sat or knelt in the bottom of the canoe, and swept it from bow to stern. You had to be quick and keep the pole going or the herrings would wriggle off." At the oilery the herring were reduced for their oil, and the refuse was dumped back into the inlet.

the Fraser's port and an important link for steamers heading up to the interior's gold mining towns and camps. It was also the setting of sawmills and a new, growing industry that traced its origins to the HBC's Fort Langley operation – salmon fishing. Instead of salting and packing the fish, entrepreneurs began packaging the fish in tin cans. One of them was Captain Edward Stamp, who, following his retirement from Stamp's Mill, turned to salmon canning in 1871. His partner was a black South Carolina native, John Sullivan Deas, a tinsmith. Stamp died the following year, but Deas persisted, opening his own cannery on a small island now named for him – Deas Island – on the Fraser. Deas' success created a new maritime industry on the Fraser; as fleets of fishing boats net-

Related to its nautical cousin, the box sextant is a late 18th century British invention for land surveying. This example dates to the mid-19th century, and was the type used on shore by military and naval officers busily engaged in surveying the colony of British Columbia. Light, portable and easier to transport, it was one of the essential tools for Colonial expansion and mapping.

Like a nautical sextant, the box sextant measures angles, but it is a smaller, enclosed version placed inside a cylindrical box. Its graduated arc is at half degrees from 0° to 120°.

The readings on its vernier were read to single minutes using a magnifying glass.

Overleaf: Three barques load 12-inch by 12-inch timbers at Hastings Mill in the late 19th century. The white-hulled barque to the left has opened bow ports for slipping the long and heavy timbers into the hold.

When the oilery failed in 1886 after the herring migration shifted and the fish stopped coming into Burrard Inlet, Spratt had the *Ark* rebuilt as a freighter. Other than a short-lived cannery built on the shores of English Bay in 1899, the era of fishing around Burrard Inlet started to fade in the face of the booming lumber business, and the urbanization of Vancouver choked off spawning streams, although the Canadian Fishing Company would build and maintain a depot for its vessels on the Inlet to offload and process fish that would last well into the 21st century.

By the late 1880s the sawmills and their surrounding settlements were now a hubbub of activity. The whine of the mills' blades echoed off the surrounding forests, and the muddy streets of the milltowns were crowded with men and women who were themselves putting down roots of a different sort in the midst of the stumps. Burrard Inlet was one of the Pacific Coast's most active lumber ports with majestic square-rigged sailing ships anchored off the mills, while other ships, stern-on to the wharves, loaded timber. In 1884, the mills of Burrard Inlet exported 24 million board feet of rough lumber, 2.2 million feet of milled lumber and a million feet of pickets in forty-three vessels. The area would have grown, albeit at a slow pace, into a great lumber port city in time, but in 1885, the decision by the Canadian Pacific Railway to terminate its transcontinental railroad at Granville changed the fortunes of both the settlements and the port.

The results were dramatic. Granville, a settlement of a hundred buildings and several hundred people, blossomed with boomtown rapidity. Within six months more than a thousand buildings stood on the site of what would soon become the "City of Vancouver" in 1886, and the population grew as rapidly as the buildings sprang up. Even a disastrous fire that leveled the new city on June 13, 1886, could not hinder the enthusiastic rise of Vancouver. While lumber remained an important export, the arrival of the CPR's trains and ships at Vancouver – where the rails met the sea – made the new "Terminal City" an important link in global maritime trade. Goods from the Far East – the age-old dream realized at last – flowed into Canada from ships that arrived at the CPR dock. Vancouver had become the gateway to the Orient.

Real Estate Office
Big Tree. Copyright applied for

Chapter Three

RAILS MEET THE SEA

1887–1913

THE DREAM OF A NORTHWEST PASSAGE had brought European mariners to the coast a century earlier. What they had not found, what did not in fact exist here, was now being artificially created, in an age of iron, steel and steam, by man. This creation would bring the silks and other riches of the Far East rapidly to Britain and its colonies. The railroad would also, as historian W. Kaye Lamb noted, "in conjunction with steamers on the Atlantic and Pacific . . . provide an all-British Route" not only to Asia and Australasia, but also as the final link for British steamship service that circled the globe.

This badge belonged to Carl Timms, who started with the Canadian Pacific Railway's BC Coast Service in the early years of the 20th century. Mr. Timms worked his way up in the BCCS from Cabin Boy to Chief Steward. This was Mr. Timms' employee identification badge that he wore throughout his career.

In 1879, the Canadian Pacific Railway declared that the new transcontinental railroad, then under construction, would terminate at the end of Burrard Inlet in the "snug harbour" of Port Moody. Named for Col. Richard Moody of the Royal Engineers, who had laid out the first trail to the inlet's terminus in hope that it would grow into a protected anchorage for the Royal Navy, Port Moody now seemed destined to outshine the burgeoning settlements farther down the inlet. A government wharf, built to accommodate the ships that would soon arrive, arose on the flats, and in March 1883, the ship *Duke of Abercorn*, chartered by the CPR and laden with steel for the railroad, docked there. The port was a necessity for the ultimate success of the CPR.

In 1885, the railway's president, George Stephen, insisted that the task would not be complete "until we have an ocean connection with Japan and China."

In addition to its rolling stock and rails, the Canadian Pacific Railway needed steamships for the Atlantic, the Great Lakes and the Pacific. Eager to enter the trade, the CPR chartered ships from the firm of Frazar & Company to ship Japanese tea and other goods to Port Moody. The first ship to reach Port Moody was the American barque *W.B. Flint*, which arrived on July 27, 1886, not long after the first CPR train had rolled to a stop on the Port Moody waterfront. Longshoremen laboured to unload quickly *Flint*'s cargo of 17,430 half-chests of tea and load them on the train, which rolled out to deliver the tea to consignees in Toronto, Hamilton, Chicago and New York. Forty-nine days after *W.B. Flint* sailed from Yokohama, the last of its cargo reached New York, a record that even the fastest ship could not beat.

Port Moody's fortunes seemed assured as more chartered ships arrived to discharge their cargoes into waiting railcars. But the CPR was not happy with Port Moody. The "snug harbour" was too confined and shallow, and to reach it, ships had to navigate the length of Burrard Inlet, threading their way through two narrows that were difficult to navigate in the full force of the tide. *The British Columbia Coast Pilot*, first published in 1888, warned mariners: "you must be

The CPR's first train arrives at Port Moody. Originally touted as Canada's new Pacific port, Port Moody lost out to its new rival, Vancouver, in 1885.

Overleaf: The CPR chartered barque *W.B. Flint* offloads its cargo of half-chests of tea from the Orient at Port Moody on July 28, 1886.

The crew engagement register for the CPR steamer *Empress of India*, dated December 14, 1900. The master was Captain O.P. Marshall and the First Officer/Mate was Edward Beetham. This register was the legal listing of the crew and records their names, addresses, nationality, age and rate of pay.

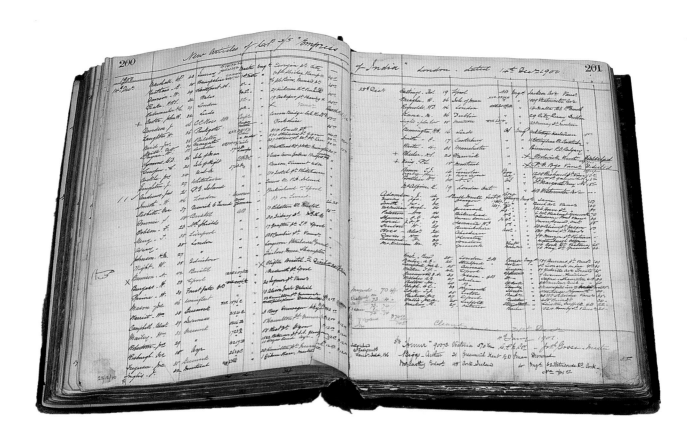

quick and careful with the helm. Even for a steam-vessel the strength of the streams in First Narrows necessitates unusual care."

One of the CPR's chartered ships learned the hard way when she grounded on a shoal just inside the Narrows off Brockton Point in 1890. To this day, "Parthia Shoal" carries the name of the steamship that grounded and then got off. Then there was the problem of real estate. Sharp speculators had snapped up much of Port Moody's waterfront property in anticipation of making a fortune with the CPR-inspired boom. That was counter to the CPR's own interests; they wanted the profit margin from the sale of real estate, particularly to industries that would require rail service.

Even as Port Moody's residents and speculators planned for a lucrative future, CPR officials met secretly with the premier of British Columbia to secure the rights to public lands and waterfront next to tiny Granville and Hastings Mill. The CPR's eyes had been on Granville since as early as 1884, when the railway's general manager, William Van Horne, suggested that Granville change its name to "Vancouver." Van Horne saw value in the worldwide recognition of the name – not necessarily of the explorer and navigator, but of the island that now bore his surname. Investors, shippers and mariners around the world knew of Vancouver Island, far more than Burrard Inlet or Granville, and so the

The CPR's locomotive #374 arrives in Vancouver on May 23, 1887. The first transcontinental train to reach Vancouver, it is greeted by a welcoming crowd who appreciate that the port's future success is assured by the rail link across Canada and the ocean link to the Pacific Rim and the rest of the world.

city received a new name. In 1887, with vast tracts of what would be prime real estate turned over to the company, the CPR shifted its operation to Vancouver and the skid road port that lay on its shores. With the rails extended along Burrard Inlet's southern shore to Coal Harbour, where a new dock, built out from the elevated banks of the inlet, and a dockside passenger station and freight warehouse now stood, Vancouver was about to be transformed from a skid road port into a thriving entrepôt.

Meanwhile, the CPR had shifted from the wooden ships of Frazar & Company to three veteran iron-hulled steamers it chartered from the Cunard Line. *Abyssinia*, *Parthia* and *Batavia*, nearing the end of their

second decade afloat, formed the genesis of the CPR's Pacific fleet as the company negotiated with the British government for a contract to carry the mail, and a resultant subsidy for constructing steamers of its own. *Abyssinia*, the first to reach Vancouver, arrived three weeks after the first train had rolled into town on May 23, 1887. On June 14th, just thirteen days, fourteen hours out of Yokohama, *Abyssinia* docked at Vancouver with 102 passengers (80 of them Chinese), tea, general merchandise, "curios" and the inlet's first load of raw silk. Hastily unloaded and sent on its way, the steamer's cargo was transshipped back east, with a "small trial parcel" that was rushed to New York, loaded on a steamer and sent to London, arriving

This lightly built wooden and paper-covered tea caddy, one of the many Asian commodities shipped aboard the CPR's *Empresses* to a North American and European market, is a rare surviving example of these ornate but fragile "throw-away" crates.

twenty-nine days after it left Yokohama. It was, as W. Kaye Lamb would later comment, a "sensational record."

Abyssinia, *Parthia* and *Batavia* made regular voyages to and from Vancouver and the Orient, usually fully loaded with tea, rice, silk and other merchandise and contingents of just over a hundred passengers. They initially carried little when leaving Vancouver. The lumber trade, still active, was carried to markets in sailing ships that, even in the triumphant age of the steamship, carried bulk cargoes cheaply and competitively. With as many as sixty or more ships calling at Vancouver and Moodyville each year to load lumber, the chartered CPR steamers departed with smaller outbound

cargoes than they had arrived with, although gradually a trade in flour developed.

The flour was not a BC product, but the product of Oregon mills shipped up the coast from Portland. It was closer, faster and cheaper for the Oregonians to send their flour north across the international border than south to San Francisco and the vessels of the American-owned Pacific Mail Steamship Company and the Oriental & Occidental Line. Until Japanese steamship lines linked up with American railroad interests and commenced running out of Puget Sound in 1896, the CPR's steamers had a monopoly on the North Pacific run to Asia, carrying American flour and cotton.

When the CPR finally signed a mail

These dinner chimes from an *Empress* steamship of the CPR were rung by hand by the ship's stewards to call passengers to dinner.

contract with the government in the summer of 1889, a subsidy was now available to build three new steamers that would carry the Royal Mail and serve as auxiliary cruisers in the Royal Navy in the event of war. Built in England, *Empress of India*, *Empress of China* and *Empress of Japan* were near sisters. Painted brightly, the "White Empresses" inaugurated a new era for the CPR. *Empress of India* was first to arrive in the Pacific, steaming around the world by way of the Suez Canal, Hong Kong, Shanghai, Nagasaki and Kobe. She arrived in Vancouver on April 28, 1891, with 1,810 tons of tea, silk, rice and opium and 486 passengers. By the end of the year the other two steamers had joined her.

A new record was set in August 1891,

when *Empress of Japan*, the trains and the steamer *City of New York* transferred mail from Yokohama to Vancouver to New York and then to London in only twenty-two days. Other fast trains, with specially-built cars, rushed the perishable raw silk from the ships to markets around the continent. The "silk train" became a legend, as did the ships that delivered the silk to them. Their reputation established, the *Empresses* commenced regular, clockwork sailings in and out of Vancouver that opened up new opportunities for the city and the port as the CPR's trade blossomed.

In 1893, a new line began calling in Vancouver. The Canadian-Australian Steamship Company now connected Vancouver and the rest of Canada with Sydney, aided by a government subsidy to carry the mail. The first vessel in the new service, the steamer *Miowera*, arrived at Vancouver on June 9, 1893.

One entrepreneur who saw the benefits of the new port's global and transcontinental rail connections was American-born Benjamin Tingley "B.T." Rogers. In 1890, Rogers built and opened the BC Sugar Refining Company in Vancouver, on the shores of Burrard Inlet. He did it with the backing of the CPR, who granted preferential freight rates because it was, in the words of Rogers' biographer, "eager for economic development to anchor its western terminal." Civic officials agreed to purchase the land for his refinery and waive

The CPR's second-generation Pacific
liner *Empress of Asia*, circa 1911.
This beautiful watercolour by
C.F. Clement captures the Empress

Empress of India steams past the broken remnants of the steamer *Beaver*, circa 1891. For several years the wreck of the pioneer steamboat remained visible off the shores of Prospect Point, a reminder of the old days and the humble beginnings of the port.

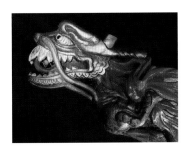

Top: The original wood-carved dragon figurehead of *Empress of Japan* (1). A copy stands in Stanley Park; the original, now restored, is displayed in the Vancouver Maritime Museum.

Top right: This brass and steel straight razor (sometimes called a "cut throat" razor) is specially engraved; it belonged to *Empress of Japan* (1)'s hairdresser M. Brurein,

and it lists his name, title and the ship's name. The style and elegance of the age is exemplified in something as small and yet as exquisite as this razor.

Bottom: The Canadian Pacific Railway produced beautiful menus, passenger lists and advertising materials for their liners, like these for the first and second generation Pacific steamships.

Opposite: Raw sugar, packed in large wicker baskets, arrives in Vancouver for processing at B.T. Rogers' BC Sugar Refinery on the shores of Burrard Inlet.

the first fifteen years' taxes. Ships brought raw sugar from the Philippines and Fiji, discharging it at Rogers' wharf. The final product, packaged in bags, was then shipped to market on the CPR's trains.

The first years of the refinery were difficult ones, including a disastrous loss of two ships, their crews and cargoes of raw sugar in late 1892 and early 1893. The ship *Morayshire* sailed from Java for Vancouver with 2,100 tons in October 1892 and was never heard from again. The next ship to load for Vancouver, *Blair Athole*, sailed from Java with 2,326 tons in March 1893. Amazingly and tragically, *Blair Athole* also disappeared. It was a terrible loss both in terms of lives and money, particularly when

coupled with fierce competition from Victoria, Montreal and California-based rivals. Despite the tough times, BC Sugar survived and ultimately thrived, particularly when the Klondike Gold Rush drove up sugar prices. Vancouver and its new port were hard hit by the economic recession of 1892–1897, and it was not until gold was discovered in the Yukon that the city and port's fortunes revived along with those of industries like Rogers'. As Canada's "gateway to the Klondike" (a name it shared with rivals Victoria and Seattle), Vancouver found prosperity again in the winter of 1897–98 as hundreds of miners and tons of provisions headed north on a variety of craft from old sailing ships to steamers.

This seaman's discharge certificate, dated April 13, 1900, rates *Empress of Japan*'s Jr. Third Engineer Harry Burgess "VG" for very good ability and conduct, ensuring he could be hired again.

The octant or quadrant was a primary navigational aid in the measurement of altitude at sea. Invented by John Hadley around 1731, within ten years it was in general production worldwide. Modified and adapted to function with optics within thirty years, it was renamed a sextant and, in its modern version, is still standard nautical equipment. This octant, with two peepholes for sighting, possibly dates from early 1800s.

The barque *Camsbusdoon*, one of the many sugar carriers that sailed into Vancouver. She made a 183-day voyage to the port from Java in 1896. The days of working sail were ending as steamers replaced them. Old ships like *Camsbusdoon* were now "tramps" carrying bulk freight at a slow speed for low rates.

Rogers' sugar refinery was not the only new business to rise on the shores of Burrard Inlet and its surrounding waters that owed its success to the arrival of the CPR in Vancouver. Initially settled by a single mill in 1886, False Creek now came into prominence as an industrial centre. Sawmills, shingle mills, a cooperage and the boat-building yards of Andy Linton and shipyard of Alfred Wallace ringed the tidal flats of the creek by the mid 1890s. The Granville Street Bridge, the first to span the Creek in 1889, was augmented by the Cambie Street Bridge in 1891, and in 1902 the CPR built a rail bridge across the creek's mouth. False Creek continued to industrialize; by 1910, more than twenty businesses stood on its shores.

The businesses and industries, particularly the mills and Wallace's yard, used the water, but it was the CPR's rails and cars that served many of the machine shops and other businesses along the creek. Despite these new developments, historian William McKee notes, "Vancouver never emerged as a major industrial centre. To this day, it continues to operate primarily as an entrepôt."

Vancouver was a maritime hub where goods and people arrived by sea daily and were then redistributed by rail or on to other vessels, to the interior or up and down the coast. Located as it was on the Inside Passage, Vancouver was in a perfect position to become the major port for ships running to the logging camps, canneries

Paul Goranson
BC Pursue Seiners, circa 1940

Paul Goranson's etching depicts
the hard, old-fashioned way of
hauling in a net full of fish in the
days before power blocks and
hydraulic equipment. In this
fashion over half a decade the
waters of the Fraser and the Gulf
of Georgia were harvested.

"BC Purse Seiners"   12/60

Paul Goranson '40

The Fraser River steamer *Enterprise*. Built at San Francisco in 1861 for service on California's Sacramento River, the sternwheeler headed north when purchased by the Hudson's Bay Company in 1862 to run between New Westminster and Victoria. *Enterprise* remained in service until rammed by the steamer *R.P. Rithet* off Victoria on July 28, 1885. *Enterprise*, laden with cattle, freight and 50 passengers from New Westminster, sank with a loss of two lives. Salvagers recovered the steamer's machinery, including this gauge, but left the hull to the sea. It remained visible until 1905.

and other settlements that were springing up along the passage on the various inlets and islands. Starting in the 1850s, the Hudson's Bay Company's steamers *Otter*, *Labouchere* and *Enterprise* had run up and down the coast, carrying passengers and freight out of Victoria.

The Canadian Pacific Navigation Company, formed in 1883 by veteran New Westminster mariner Captain John Irving, picked up that business from the HBC. Irving had built up his reputation following in his father William's footsteps after the family immigrated to British Columbia during the Fraser River gold rush. First running between Victoria and New Westminster and after 1862 up the river

from New Westminster to Yale, William Irving had been the most successful and best known Fraser River steamboat captain, earning the title "King of the River." When he died in 1872, his son John, who joined his father's business at age sixteen in 1870, assumed a greater role and emerged as the preeminent steamer operator on the BC coast and the river by the early 1880s. His new company, made up of vessels from his own Pioneer Line and the HBC's old *Enterprise* after he bought out the Bay's interests in coastal shipping, became the principal line to work the BC coast and the various settlements and towns growing up along the Fraser River. The river, now developing into a major fishery, was dotted with canneries. It also served an agricultural heartland with its own major river port at New Westminster as the hub for the river valley's farming interests.

In the late 1880s, Irving bought two new steel-hulled vessels, *Premier* and *Islander*. By the end of the century, his flourishing business attracted the interest of the Canadian Pacific Railway, and in 1901 the CPR bought Irving's fleet in an effort to corner the coastal trade. The CPR focused its attention on steamship service between Vancouver and Victoria, south to the Puget Sound port of Seattle, and north to the Alaskan ports of Ketchikan, Sitka and Juneau. It operated with Irving's old boats until March 1903, when its first purpose-built steamer, the 300-foot (91-metre)

Captain John Irving's cap badge from his Canadian Pacific Navigation Company uniform.

Princess Victoria, arrived on the coast. The CPR rapidly added to their fleet of "Princesses," as well as interior lake steamers, steam tugs and ocean steamers; in 1910, a company poster listed sixty-five vessels in the company's "steamship fleets," forty-two of them operating in British Columbia.

Another coastwise company, the first steamship line based in Vancouver, came into existence in 1889. The Union Steamship Company was established to serve northern communities, large and small, beginning with three small steam tugs, *Senator*, *Leonora* and *Skidegate*, that carried some passengers. The company bought the 180-foot (54-metre) steamer *Cutch* in 1890, running her between Vancouver and Nan-

aimo until the Klondike Gold Rush. Sent north in 1898, *Cutch* lasted for ten years before wrecking. In 1901, Union rebuilt the burnt-out sailing ship *J.R. MacDonald* into the steamer *Cassiar*, which made about 1,700 voyages before retirement in 1923. With a fleet of some sixty vessels of its own, Union Steamships was a formidable rival to the CPR. The Union Steamships established themselves as public favourites – workaday boats, running to logging camps, canneries and steamer landings with provisions, the mail, school teachers, loggers, fishermen and cannery workers, "working girls," doctors and others, blowing their whistles to let everyone in the vicinity know that they were approaching the wharf, pier or float. With the Union Boats and wharf near the CPR's docks, Vancouver had become more than a lumber port and the Canadian Pacific Railway's terminus.

THE ACTIVE DEVELOPMENT of Vancouver, New Westminster and their surrounding communities, all linked by water, included the construction of waterfront facilities and significant steps taken by the government to aid navigation. The active Gold Rush traffic on the Fraser in the late 1850s had highlighted the need to mark a safe passage through the hazardous entrance to the river. Six years after the first petition to the government, the channel at South Sand Heads (off the river's mouth near modern Steveston) was marked by a lightship in

A rare view...the CPR steamer *Princess Victoria* arrives in March 1903 without a wooden superstructure. Local boatbuilders added this to the steamer before she commenced service.

Delta, built in Victoria in 1889, worked as a cannery tender. Shown here alongside two heavily laden fish scows on the Fraser, she remained afloat as a houseboat on her 100th birthday, having survived a long career in the fishing industry.

Overleaf: The Union Steamship Company's coastal liner *Venture* (2) heads up the coast, stuffed with freight, baggage, and cannery workers heading north for the season. Many workers were First Nations people, such as these women and children on the deck.

The former pilot boat and sealing schooner *Thomas F. Bayard*, moored off Steveston as the lightship *Sandheads No.16*. It remained on station for forty-two years. Note the light atop the foremast.

1865. In 1879, a screw-pile-supported lighthouse replaced the by then rotten hulk, and it, in turn, was replaced by an old sealer converted into a lightship in 1905. That vessel only lasted until 1912, when, leaking, it was also replaced by a thirty-two-year-old former sealer and pilot boat named *Thomas F. Bayard*.

Renamed *Sandheads No. 16*, the "new" lightship marked the Fraser entrance for the next forty-two years. The major government investments in the river, however, were the construction of stone jetties to help tame the entrance beginning in 1909, and municipally and federally funded harbour improvements at New Westminster between 1910 and 1912. These improvements finally made the Fraser-side city a deepwater port, a dream of the mid-19th

century hitherto thwarted by the river's shoals and the rise of Vancouver.

On Burrard Inlet, the first lighthouse, erected at Point Atkinson, was not completed until 1875 because the wrong light had been sent and needed replacing. The low wooden tower was an isolated station for its first keepers, who relied on a small rowboat to commute to Vancouver for needed supplies. The work was difficult not only for the keepers but also for their families. The wives of many lighthouse keepers were themselves unrecognized and uncompensated "keepers" labouring to keep the lights going while raising children in isolation and occasional privation.

The wreck of the steamer *Beaver* in 1888 compelled the government to erect a light at Prospect Point in newly that same fall. In 1890, the government built another light inside the First Narrows at Brockton Point. The keeper's duties included aiding those in peril in addition to the maintenance and operation of the light and nearby fog signal. On July 21, 1906, Vancouver witnessed its worst shipwreck when the CPR's *Princess Victoria* rammed and sank the tiny Union Steamship *Chehalis*, which had crossed the larger steamer's bow. As horrified passengers on *Princess Victoria* watched, the tiny wooden steamer was crushed and chopped up by their ship's propellers. Out of fifteen aboard *Chehalis*, only eight survived, plucked from the cold water by Brockton Point lighthouse keeper William Jones.

WORKERS ON THE WATERFRONT

The most important workers on the waterfront were the longshoremen and stevedores who were responsible for the discharging and loading of ships. The first longshoremen worked alongside ships' crews to load the lumber ships that called at Burrard Inlet. It was not steady work, and the early longshoremen worked as mill hands, loggers, fishermen and labourers when there were no ships in port. Many of them were from the Squamish nation; others were seamen who had left the sea to live ashore, and who knew how to handle a ship's rigging to sling cargo in and out of holds—or to rig heavy timbers to slide into lumber ports at the ship's stern when long cuts of lumber would not fit into a hatch.

One pioneering longshore-man, Paddy Coyle, recalled that when he arrived in Vancouver as a seaman and decided to stay and work the docks, "We lined up alongside the ship and got picked. We worked 10 hours a day and got 35¢ an hour and 40¢ overtime."

The arrival of the CPR and growth of the port changed the nature and the pace of work. Larger, more diverse cargoes, especially the teas and silks that had to be rapidly discharged from the "Empresses" and loaded on the trains for fast shipment east, required a professional dockside labour force. The CPR's reputation for speedy transits of cargoes from the Orient was based just as much on the skills and hard work of Vancouver's longshoremen. The work was often backbreaking. Another pioneer, Harry Walters,

recalled unloading 250-pound (114-kilogram) sacks of raw sugar at the Rogers refinery. Two men would hoist a sack and place it on a gravity powered dolly that ran from the dock to the refinery and then back again. "The sacks used to stick together and the men below had spuds [wooden poles] to pry them apart. That was a tough job. No let up."

The construction of more docks, and the increasing pace of arrivals led to the creation of small stevedoring firms, then larger ones. In 1904, the Victoria and Vancouver Stevedoring Company commenced work, followed in 1910 by the Empire Stevedoring Company. After 1911, both Victoria and Vancouver Stevedoring and Empire controlled much of the work on the waterfront.

Attempts to organize the waterfront workers began in 1888 when a number of longshoremen joined the newly established local of the short-lived Knights of Labor, an American trade union formed in 1869 that was spreading around the continent. In 1896, some eighty longshoremen formed their own union, but after a prolonged and bitter strike against the CPR, the union folded. A new union of lumber handlers sprang up in North Vancouver in 1906, and soon linked itself with the Industrial Workers of the World (IWW). It was not until 1912 that Vancouver's longshoremen made another attempt to organize. This time it was successful. On March 30, 1912, the Vancouver Local of the International Longshoremens Association (ILA) was formed with sixty charter members. The lumber handlers of the IWW merged with the ILA, and as historian William McKee has noted, "the foundations of modern labour relations had been laid on the Vancouver waterfront."

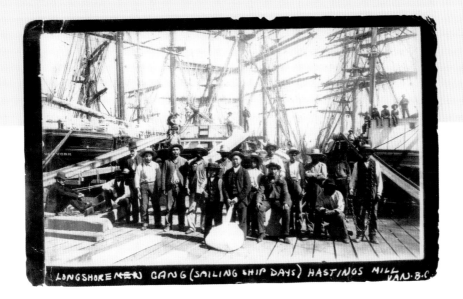

LONGSHOREMEN GANG (SAILING SHIP DAYS) HASTINGS MILL VAN.B.C

Longshoremen at Hastings Mill in the 1880s, largely made of up of members of the Squamish Nation, who formed many of the inlet's early stevedoring and longshoring crews. Standing with the crew is a Chinese laundryman with his sack of laundry.

Maritime traffic on Burrard Inlet was safer than the tragic accident of *Chehalis* would suggest despite the busy port. Ferry service across the inlet had improved since the first rowboats and tiny steamers of milltown days, although some old-timers fondly recalled the unsafe but humorous (in hindsight) steam scow and ferry *Union*. Known as the "Sudden Jerk," *Union*'s crew usually stopped her by throwing an old sack into the engine's gears or simply ramming the dock. Other entrepreneurs offered improved, albeit less colourful service, although, as historian Doreen Armitage notes, "gregarious" Captain Hugh Stalker of the ferry *Senator*, "set a congenial atmosphere for the passengers, who often

Built on a scow hull in 1873, and powered by a locomotive boiler and a threshing machine, the short-lived Burrard Inlet ferry *Union* ("Sudden Jerk") ended her days when a spark set a load of hay on fire and she burned on the Fraser in 1878.

followed him ashore at Hastings Mill and continued their conversations at the bar at the Alhambra Hotel."

The 19th century ended with the new city of Vancouver assuming a new identity as Canada's Pacific Coast metropolis, replacing Victoria as British Columbia's principal port of entry. New steamship lines established themselves in the first decade of the new 20th century. They continued to link Vancouver with its coastal neighbours and trade opportunities in the United States and across the Pacific. In 1901, seventy-one ocean-going ships called at Vancouver. Four years later, 132 ships, nearly double that number, steamed through the Lions Gate. Among them were the ships of the Pacific Coast Steamship Company, connecting Vancouver with Alaska and San Francisco, the Canadian-Australian lines' steamers, the "Empresses" and "Princesses" of the CPR, the "Union Boats," and an uncounted number of smaller tugs, barges, scows and fishing boats that regularly called.

The fishing industry, dominated by two Vancouver-based companies, had expanded beyond the limits of the Fraser. While forty-eight canneries now stood on the banks of the Fraser, others were located along the coast, and as the number of canneries had grown, so too had the fishing fleet. Steveston, at the mouth of the Fraser, was Canada's west coast fishing capital; its canned fish was loaded into ships that

Top: Point Atkinson Light at the entrance to Vancouver Harbour. This is the second tower, built in 1912 with reinforced concrete.

Bottom left: The second Brockton Point Light, built in 1914 to straddle the sea walk in Stanley Park.

Bottom right: The original Prospect Point Light, built in 1888 after the wreck of the *Beaver*. The large bells warned mariners on foggy days and nights. The original tower, demolished in 1948, was replaced by a modern concrete structure.

RECREATIONAL BOATING

Recreational boating on Burrard Inlet and English Bay is as old as the first mills and logging camps to rise on their shores. Mill workers rowed four-oared craft off the Hastings Mill dock in 1882 in the first known boat races on the inlet, and in June 1886 the press reported on Burrard Inlet's first sailing race, when the newly built "pleasure yacht" *Senor* raced the sloop *Marcia*. In 1886, aficionados founded the Vancouver Boating Club, and in 1887 the Burrard Inlet Sailing Club was formed, followed by the Burrard Inlet Rowing Club in 1890.

Vancouver's first commercial boat builders were Andy Linton and William Watts, the latter arriving in December 1888 with business partner Edward Trott from the east. Primarily building boats for the fledgling fishing industry, Watts and Trott also built boats for rowing clubs, with Watts avidly joining the local yachting scene as a racer as well as a builder.

In 1897, a group of local yachtsmen founded the Vancouver Yachting Club, with slips for the members at Andy Linton's float at the foot of Carrall Street in Coal Harbour. The yacht club languished and failed, and it was not until 1903, largely in response to a challenge from Seattle's yacht club, that seventeen Vancouver yachtsmen founded the Vancouver Yacht Club. Taking up quarters with the thriving Vancouver Rowing Club at Coal Harbour, the yacht club built its own clubhouse in 1904 and expanded.

In addition to the middle class who loved to go out in their boats, the new club also attracted the infant city's elite, among them sugar magnate B.T. Rogers, who joined in 1904 with the club's first power vessel, the 50-foot (15-metre) steam yacht *Mow Ping*. The club was more than just a men's organization. Women, while denied a voting membership for years, were nonetheless active participants in the RVYC's water activities. Even then, despite the prejudices of the time, the men of the RVYC admitted that some of the Club's best sailors were the "lady skippers."

In 1906, the club received the Royal Warrant and became the "Royal Vancouver Yacht Club." The Club's only major setback was when its new clubhouse, built in 1908, burned at the end of 1909, but a new structure soon arose on the shores of Coal Harbour, and by 1913, on the occasion of its tenth anniversary, the RVYC boasted a membership of 140 boats and was heralded by the Vancouver Daily Province as "the premier yacht club on the Pacific Coast of Canada."

The Vancouver Rowing Club, near the edge of Stanley Park sometime around 1910, with a few boats of the young Royal Vancouver Yacht Club moored nearby.

called at its docks or was run into Vancouver and the CPR's wharves by a railroad that linked "Salmonopolis" (as the busy and crowded settlement was now called in a nod to its rapid and impressive growth) with Burrard Inlet. Steveston prospered in the first decade of the new century, boasting a population of 10,000 and a number of urban amenities that ranged from stores and hotels to saloons and brothels.

The population of Vancouver and its immediate environs quadrupled between 1901 and 1911. The growing municipalities on the North Shore – North Vancouver and West Vancouver – also grew, and the need for commuter ferries led to a small fleet that began with the 73-foot (22-metre)

ferry *North Vancouver* in 1900, and in 1905 saw the addition of the 131-foot (39-metre) *North Vancouver Ferry No. 2*. In 1911, the City of North Vancouver took control of the ferries and added a third to the fleet. Meanwhile, ferry service to West Vancouver, begun in 1909, also passed into government control when the new municipality of West Vancouver took over that system in 1912.

In 1910, a new steamship line, founded by the CPR's rival Grand Trunk Pacific Railroad, began connecting Vancouver with Prince Rupert, BC's northernmost port and an ostensible rival. Farther south, the Panama Canal, then under construction, offered the promise of even greater growth, and the hope that Canadian grain from the prairies would pour into Vancouver and New Westminster by rail. From there it would take a fast ocean voyage by way of the new canal to European markets. The signs were auspicious, and the shipping community and their dockside partners waited for the opening of the canal in 1914 with anticipation.

Launched into service in 1900, the ferry *North Vancouver* ran between North Vancouver and Vancouver until 1925, when she was transformed into the tug *Norvan*. She ceased that operation in the 1950s and now, over a century later, still serves – as a dry-land house boat.

"Choice Fraser River" salmon,
caught and canned locally, and
shipped around the world.

The arduous duties of cannery work were often undertaken by female workers and children, many of them members of the various First Nations. Here, workers pack cans of herring at the Gulf of Georgia Cannery during the Second World War.

Chapter Four

DREAMS AND DEVELOPMENT

1914–1939   THANKS TO THE PANAMA CANAL, the second decade of the new century was full of promise for Vancouver and its surrounding cities and towns. Wheat grown on the vast plains of central Canada could at last be shipped, via the Canal, to Europe, bypassing ice-bound eastern ports in winter. In 1913, the provincial government, eager to capitalize on the potential profits, forced the sale of the Kitsilano Indian Reserve near the mouth of False Creek for a new deep-sea harbour facility. To the south, the City of Richmond, inspired by industrialist Charles Pretty, contemplated building an 8.4-square-mile (2175-hectare) freight and passenger terminal on the Georgia Strait shores of Lulu Island.

An aggressive program of dredging to deepen the channels of the Fraser, followed by the construction of jetties at the mouth of the river's south and south arms, had commenced in 1909. Buoyed by the promise of an improved river channel, New Westminster invested half a million dollars in new riverfront harbour facilities between 1910 and 1912, to which the federal government added $200,000 in 1912 to ensure New Westminster's dream of becoming "the Liverpool of the Pacific."

Federal funding was also vital for Vancouver. The Burrard Inlet port was experiencing an increase in shipping. In 1911, the Union Steamship Company of New Zealand began linking New Zealand and Vancouver, and European steamship lines – the Hamburg Amerika, Royal Mail Steam Packet and the East Asiatic companies – had established Vancouver service. Coastal traffic doubled, and Vancouver, too, had its eye on the grain trade. In June 1912, Alexander McCandless, president of the Vancouver Board of Trade, endorsed increased development of the port because "Vancouver will grow and prosper as never before . . . after the opening of the Panama Canal. Railways will fight for terminals in this city, and new sections of the country will contribute to the wealth of our beloved city."

The contribution mentioned by McCandless was wheat, and the means to handle it, sought by the Board of Trade since 1906, was a grain elevator. Ever since the CPR had arrived in town, Vancouverites had sought to divert the eastward flow of Canadian prairie grain to their new port. In June 1887, at a dinner aboard *Abyssinia*, the first CPR ship to reach Vancouver, an enthusiastic civic guest had urged the railway officials in the audience to "work up a new industry in bringing the wheat of the great North West to Vancouver, where mills could be erected to grind it, and from thence distribute to our Eastern Hemisphere. . . ." The suggestion, politely deferred by the CPR in favour of tea, silks and general merchandise, was never forgotten by Vancouver. In 1899, the city finally shipped out its first major cargoes of grain. Oats bagged in Edmonton and shipped by the CPR to Vancouver were

Commemorative plate presented to F.C. Wade, K.C., to mark the occasion of the sailing of the Swedish motorship *Buenos Aires*, "First Voyage with Canadian Grain from Vancouver, BC via the Panama Canal to the United Kingdom, 11 March 1921." The plaque is in error, as the steamer *Effingham* was the first, steaming out of Vancouver loaded with Canadian grain in January of the same year.

Longshoremen loading sacks of flour in a ship's hold on the Vancouver waterfront, 1926. Loading a ship was hard work and required skill to load it correctly to keep the ship in trim.

loaded on steamers for South Africa to feed British horses during the Boer War.

The rapid end of the Boer War doomed big profits for grain marketers, but the trade survived with wheat shipments to the Philippines, Mexico and Alaska. During 1910 and 1912, three-quarters of a million bushels of wheat left Vancouver in sacks that had to be manhandled and slung into the ships. What was needed was a means of handling the grain and wheat in bulk, offloading railcars into grain elevators that would then discharge it, in golden streams, into the holds of the waiting ships. New Westminster, Vancouver's rival, was lobbying Ottawa for a grain elevator, but it did not have as effective a voice as Vancouver's

Sling loading sacks of flour from railcars into a Japanese freighter alongside Vancouver's Terminal Dock, 1927.

Member of Parliament, Henry Herbert Stevens. Stevens, a major proponent of the port, sought federal government support, backed by municipal and provincial politicians eager to secure Ottawa's largesse for Vancouver.

Stevens successfully lobbied for the establishment of a federally appointed and funded Harbour Commission to improve and administer Burrard Inlet, English Bay, Indian Arm and False Creek's docks and harbour facilities. In May 1913, Parliament passed Stevens' bill, creating commissions not only for Burrard Inlet, but also for the North Arm of the Fraser and New Westminster, overseeing the rest of the Fraser. Each commission was formed with three commissioners, and they were empowered to hire a harbour master, port warden, shipping master, engineers and other officials to regulate navigation, shoreside development and shipping in the new ports. Thanks to Stevens' support, federal funds were also made available to start construction of a concrete "Government Wharf" in 1914, and an industrial, water and rail linked island on False Creek, soon called Granville Island, all under the auspices of the new Vancouver Harbour Commission.

Dredging the channel into the tidal slough of False Creek provided the sand fill for the island, which took shape in 1916 as a thirty-six-acre (14.4 hectare) flat formed by a million cubic yards (764 600 cubic metres) of sand and mud poured behind wooden

MASTODON

In 1909 the Dominion government ordered a dredge for Vancouver Harbour from William Simons & Co. Ltd. of Renfrew, Scotland, one of the world's pre-eminent dredge builders. Completed in 1910 as a 200-foot (60-metre) steel-hulled hopper bucket dredge, No. 508 worked by dredging with a continual belt of buckets that lifted 1,200 tons of material per hour.

In 1912, *Mastodon* steamed to Vancouver to begin a five-year project, working twenty-four hours a day to widen the First Narrows and reduce Parthia Shoal. The dredge's noisy work of hauling up rocks and breaking them into smaller rocks off the First Narrows went on six days a week, with peace only descending on the waterfront and the weary residents of the North Shore every Sunday because the dredge's master was a religious man as well as a hard worker.

Once the job at the Narrows was done, *Mastodon* moved on to dredge the channel of the Fraser River and build the jetties at its entrance. The dredging of the North Arm of the Fraser and the construction of the North Arm Jetty in 1915 tamed the channel and finally allowed the North Arm to become a primary booming ground for local sawmills.

The North Arm, under the jurisdiction of the North Fraser Port Commissioners, was now open for business.

Mastodon works at the First Narrows. This view was taken from the Prospect Point signal station, perched atop the point, which guided vessels in and out of port until the Second World War.

"Ship in B.C. Marine Drydock - Van., B.C." Orville N. Fisher
-1936- 12/30

Orville N. Fisher
Ship in BC Marine Drydock, 1936

Workers repair a steamer in BC
Marine Shipyard's dry dock on the
Vancouver waterfront.

"Bachelor's Hall," circa 1887. This float house was for employees of the CPR who worked at False Creek's Roundhouse. From these humble beginnings False Creek's waters became the industrial heart of Vancouver.

seawalls and piles by hydraulic dredges. Linked by rail and water, "Industrial Island" by 1920 was at the heart of a creek that had developed into a "back-up harbour for Burrard Inlet" and the home of dozens of companies that ranged from machine repair facilities, a coal and building supplies firm, ironworks, wire rope manufacturers, a chain forge and boilermakers. The island's businesses ultimately found that the Panama Canal's promise to link Vancouver to both commodities and market was fulfilled, albeit with some interesting and not always pleasing results for workers. Charles Turpin, a worker at British Ropes, a wire rope manufacturer on the island, later reminisced: "Our wire came from England around through the Panama Canal and up the west coast. That wire was covered with

gooey grease to keep it from rusting. And going through the Panama Canal, the bottom of the boat would get so hot that it would melt into a great glob. . . . That's the way we got it. On a real cold day, you would have to go down and melt some of that grease with a torch."

While the island repaid the new harbour commission's investment, the inlet's (and British Columbia's) first grain terminal did not. Built in 1913, it languished for the next few years. Vancouver's port, gripped by a worldwide economic depression, faltered along with New Westminster. The newly completed grain elevator, Terminal No. 1, sitting empty for the next few years, was renamed "Stevens' Folly" and "Stevens' White Elephant" by wags. Compounding the problem was the fact that grain growers could not easily be convinced to ship their product to Vancouver. What the new facility on the inlet had not done was instill confidence in British buyers that Canadian grain could withstand an ocean voyage through the same Panama Canal and Caribbean heat that had melted the grease off wire rope into a "great glob." At the end of 1918, a trial shipment of grain from Vancouver, carefully monitored by government scientists, proved that the grain could survive a three-and-half-month voyage to Europe with little damage. Scientific tests notwithstanding, it would take a few more years before enough confidence could be mustered to fill "Stevens' Folly" with grain.

Moment of confrontation: HMCS
Rainbow steams alongside *Komagata
Maru* on July 24, 1914.

THE *KOMAGATA MARU* INCIDENT

Ships also brought groups of people seeking a new life on these shores, from Black Americans who left pre-Civil War California's racism during the Fraser River Gold Rush to the Japanese fishermen who established themselves on the Fraser and the Chinese who came to build the railroad and those that followed later on the CPR's steamers. But with the flow of immigration came competition and racial tension.

The most powerful demonstration of this came in 1914 with the *Komagata Maru* incident. As historian Hugh Johnston aptly notes, it was a direct challenge to Canada's "colour bar" of exclusionary immigration policies. In May 1914, a group of 376 passengers – 340 Sikhs, 12 Hindus and 24 Muslims – organized specifically to test Canada's laws – sailed from the Orient for Vancouver on the freighter *Komagata Maru*. The ship, chartered for the voyage, had been specially fitted out to accommodate passengers instead of her usual coal cargoes. Arriving on the shores of English Bay on May 23, 1914, she and

her passengers were caught in a tug of war between the vessel's organizers and the Canadian government, which refused to let most of them land.

As hired Immigration boats with armed guards circled *Komagata Maru*, battles in the courts and the pages of the news papers played out for more than two months. The passengers endured extreme discomfort, privation and government harassment, which escalated over time. In the early morning hours of July 19, 1914, the tug *Sea Lion*, with thirty-five specially deputized immigration officers, armed with rifles borrowed from the Seaforth Highlanders Regiment, and accompanied by a contingent of 125 Vancouver Police officers, approached *Komagata Maru* to force the vessel from Vancouver harbour. As *Sea Lion* approached, the passengers aboard *Komagata Maru* awoke and, enraged, were ready to resist any effort to board their ship.

Manning the rail, an armed group shouted and threatened to board the tug if she made fast. Nonetheless, *Sea Lion*'s captain

brought her in close, grappled and then tied on. Passengers and police then battled as one man with an axe chopped at *Sea Lion*'s line. Using the tug's pumps and a fire hose, the police opened up with a cold stream of water. As Hugh Johnston notes, though, "the advantage was only momentary because the hose would not take the full pressure of the pumps, and the passengers were prepared with piles of coal, fire bricks, and scrap metal which they had brought up from the hold. They stood five metres above the deck of the *Sea Lion* and with that advantage loosed an unanswerable storm on the people below."

Several police officers were hit, one knocked unconscious, and others cut. The missiles smashed all the windows in the tug, cutting the faces of several men, including the tug's captain. As the police

moved to avoid the missiles, the tug listed dangerously as men shouted for order and to pull away. Finally, as a gunman aboard the ship opened fire on the tug, the line was cut and the tug retreated "looking as if it had run under a coal chute."

The government's answer was to send in the naval vessel HMCS *Rainbow* to evict *Komagata Maru* from the harbour at gunpoint. The ship finally sailed on July 23, escorted out by *Rainbow* and *Sea Lion*. The handling of the *Komagata Maru* affair was a major embarrassment for the Canadian government, as well as a cause célèbre for the Indian community and India itself. The inequality of Canada's immigration system took many decades to be redressed. To this day, the name of the ship evokes powerful memories and emotions.

Canadian officials board *Komagatu Maru* during the two-month long standoff in Vancouver Harbour.

Workers at Wallace's fit the propeller of the Imperial Munitions Board's steamer *War Dog* during the First World War.

Opposite: The massive timber frames of a *Mabel Brown* schooner rise from the ways of the Wallace Shipyards in North Vancouver. The five-masted *Mabel Brown* gave her name to a class of sister ships built during the First World War as "emergency ships."

The declaration of war on August 4, 1914 had a profound impact on the new ports. The great hopes of the Panama Canal had not yet materialized. When the canal opened in 1914, the clouds of war were already gathering in Europe, and with hostilities came a diversion of ships to the Atlantic in order to convoy troops, munitions and supplies to the theatres of war. The result, according to waterfront reporter and historian Captain James Hamilton, was "all Pacific Coast services were gradually starved out of existence, or practically so." Although economic recession still had the coast in its grip, in 1915 Vancouver received its first war commission with a two-million-dollar contract to manufacture munitions. However, the major industrial activity of the war was shipbuilding. By 1916, the

Canadian government, realizing the economic hardships, and pressed to build more ships to offset the losses to German U-Boat action, provided subsidies to West Coast shipyards to turn to war production.

On Burrard Inlet, the veteran shipbuilding firm of Alfred Wallace, relocated from False Creek to the North Shore in 1903, received a contract in 1916 to build six wooden-hulled, five-masted motor schooners. Anachronistic – most builders including Wallace had shifted to iron and then steel decades earlier – the wood, locally cut and milled Douglas Fir, was not a strategic war material. Readily available, it and wartime need dictated a return to the old ways. Retired shipwrights were called out to train men who had never worked with wood, and illustrated manuals for wooden shipbuilding, hastily published to aid the cause, were distributed. The large wooden schooners were named, as a class, after the first to clear Wallace's ways. *Mabel Brown* slid into Burrard Inlet on January 20, 1917. These schooners were the harbingers of a shipbuilding boom.

Wallace shifted back to steel and built three 315-foot (94.5-metre) steamers named *War Dog*, *War Storm* and *War Power* for the Imperial Munitions Board. Other yards sprang up to handle additional contracts. The False Creek steel firm of John Coughlan and Sons built a shipyard from the ground up on the mudflats of the Creek and began construction on 8,800-ton steel

Top: The shipyard crew poses in front of wooden-hulled freighters rising from the ways of Western Canada Shipyard on False Creek in July 1918. These vessels were destined for Europe, but the end of the war was coming, and the era of wooden steamers had passed.

Bottom: *Geraldine Wolvin*, a 1,474-ton *Mabel Brown*-type schooner built by Wallace at North Vancouver in 1917, departs the harbour with a load of lumber.

This caulking mallet, maul and slick were used by shipwrights at Wallace's to build the *Mabel Brown* schooners. The slick shaped timbers, the maul drove home drifts that held the timbers together, and the caulking mallet packed oakum (hemp and tar) into the seams of planks.

This ornate silver and tortoise shell casket, with a representation of the ship, holds the ceremonial hatchet used to launch the Canadian Pacific Railway steamer *Montcalm* at Glasgow's John Brown Shipyard on July 3, 1920. Despite BC's burgeoning shipyards and the rise of local shipbuilding during the First World War, the CPR built its ships at older, more established Scottish yards for better prices.

The hatchet, made of gilded bronze and ivory, was held by Lady Fisher, who used it to cut a thread that held back a champagne bottle. Released by the thread, the bottle crashed into the bow to christen *Montcalm*.

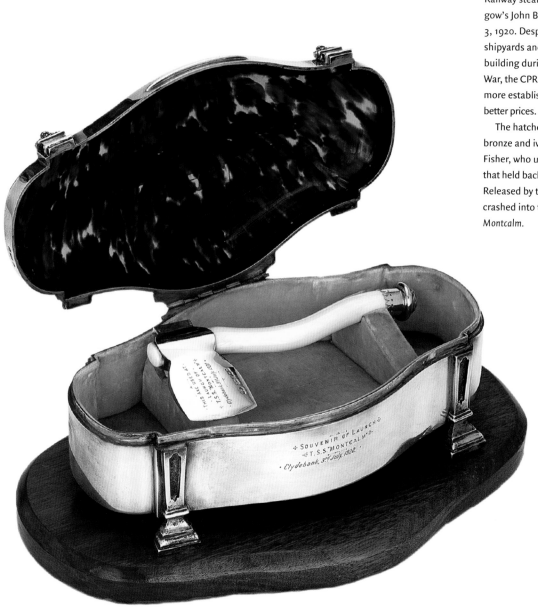

steamships and forty-five steel steamers. This represented one-third of Canada's total wartime production of cargo ships.

Unfortunately, when the boom faded, so did the shipbuilding industry. Between 1918 and 1923, employment at BC's shipyards shrank from 7,155 to 1,026 workers. Coughlan, Lyall, Northern Construction, New Westminster Construction and Pacific Construction closed, but BC Marine remained open. William Watts, who had not participated in the big boom, but steadily kept producing local craft, survived the bust and kept his Vancouver Shipyard open on Coal Harbour's shores, along with several other builders who by the 1920s had turned Coal Harbour into a bustling centre of wooden boatbuilding.

Alfred Wallace's yard, now renamed Burrard Dry Dock, also survived, helped along by a contract from the CPR's British Columbia coastal service for the 4,200-ton coaster, *Princess Louise*. It was the first time the CPR had ordered one of its vessels from a local yard. Government contracts also helped. In 1928, Burrard Dry Dock built a wooden motor schooner for the Royal Canadian Mounted Police to work in the Canadian Arctic. Christened *St. Roch*, the staunch wooden vessel would go on to make history as the second vessel ever to navigate the Northwest Passage, the first ship to circumnavigate the continent and as a twenty-year veteran of many long and arduous voyages into the frozen north.

Builders plaque from BC Marine Engineers & Shipbuilders, later BC Marine Railways. The company opened in Victoria and Vancouver in 1898. It closed in 1986 after nearly a century as a major presence in the coast's maritime operations.

steamers. Other yards also emerged such as William Lyall Shipbuilding in North Vancouver, Western Canada Shipyards Limited, BC Marine, the Pacific Construction Company and the New Westminster Construction Company.

While shipbuilding had started on the shores of the inlet in the 1870s, and local builders like William Watts and Alfred Wallace had built scores of fishing boats, tugs and coastal steamers, it was not until the war that large, oceangoing deep water ships were launched from local yards. Because of the staggering number of wartime sinkings, Wallace, Coughlan and others were kept busy through 1921. In all, British Columbia's shipyards built $88 million worth of ships – 135 vessels in all, including eighteen "Mabel Browns," sixty-nine wooden

The grain trade finally took off in 1921. On January 7, the steamer *Effingham*, loaded with a free cargo of 2,048 tons of Alberta grain, sailed from Vancouver for London, by way of the Panama Canal. Following this voyage, and with British confidence in grain shipments from Vancouver in place (not to mention a skyrocketing postwar demand for the product), Vancouver and then New Westminster gained new prominence as grain ports. As the Harbour Commissioners noted, the ultimate success of the Panama Canal "has made possible a very much lower ocean freight rate than was formerly available between Europe and the Pacific Coast and this has resulted in a large proportion of the import require-

ment of Western Canada as a whole being brought in via Vancouver instead of, as formerly, via the Atlantic Coast ports."

The first shipments of 1921 had been less than 500,000 bushels. But the dam had broken, and those amounts increased dramatically. As the trade grew, more elevators and terminals rose on the shores of the inlet. One vote of confidence in the port's new trade came when Alberta wheat farmers, eager to capture some of the profit, financed and built their own terminal, the Alberta Wheat Pool Elevator, which opened in 1929. Several years into the new trade, the "tide of golden grain" reached 95 million bushels in the twelve-month period between August 1928 and end of July 1929, fifty percent of the total cargo shipped out of Vancouver in that period. Vancouver and its rail-fed rival Prince Rupert handled twenty-eight percent of Canadian grain produced in 1929, most of it shipped to the U.K., the Orient and South America. The trade grew further as flour also started to flow out of the port. By 1930, large shipments of flour headed out past the Lions Gate for China, Japan, Hong Kong, the Philippines, New Zealand and to the smallest customer for milled flour, the United Kingdom.

The grain trade transformed the Vancouver waterfront. "Stevens' Folly," now vindicated, was joined by seven additional grain elevators capable of holding 14,550,000 bushels. Their capacity, and the steady feed of grain by rail from Alberta, Saskatchewan

Effingham loading grain prior to sailing from Vancouver on January 7, 1921, inaugurated the export of Prairie grain through the Panama Canal.

Stevedores take a rest during the backbreaking work of loading sacks of
flour aboard a freighter at Vancouver's
Terminal Dock in 1926.

The Canadian Pacific Railway's newly-built Mission Revival Pier B-C in 1927. Built for the trans-pacific *Empresses*, the pier stood until demolished for Expo 86. The modern Canada Place stands on the original CPR pilings.

Opposite: The log barge *Pacific Gatherer* (ex-sailing ship *William Dollar*) wedged beneath the Second Narrows Bridge on September 19, 1930. An error by the barge master caused the collision as *Pacific Gatherer*, under tow by the tug *Lorne*, passed the span. When the tide rose, the span tore free and fell into the inlet, and North Vancouver was cut off from rail traffic for nearly four years.

and Manitoba meant that by 1930 Vancouver could ship out as much as one hundred million bushels in a season. By the mid-1930s, according to urban historian Graeme Wynn, Vancouver was handling "more export tonnage than any harbour in Canada. Two-thirds and more of this traffic was wheat." A quarter of Canadian wheat production poured into Vancouver by rail and out again in ships. Vancouver's grain elevators could now hold eighteen million bushels of wheat, "nearly double the capacity of all the elevators on the West Coast of the United States."

The new elevators were just part of the port of Vancouver's phenomenal growth between 1918 and 1930 when the city and its surroundings municipalities expanded to some 300,000 people. New piers and

docks were part of sixty million dollars worth of improvements in that twelve-year span. The early 1920s saw the construction by the Harbour Commissioners of a new 1,200-foot (360-metre)-long covered cargo facility at Ballantyne Pier, which opened in 1923 to the Harbour Board's boast that it was "one of the most substantial, commodious, and best equipped piers in the world." The CPR built a magnificent new passenger terminal at the foot of Burrard Street, Pier B-C, in 1927. Other new docks and waterfront roads dramatically changed the Vancouver waterfront, even as another severe economic depression hit. By 1931, sixty-two vessels at any one time could berth in Vancouver.

A shoreline railroad to handle cargo, laid down on the south and then north shores, was started in 1924–25. With the rails came the first bridge to span Burrard Inlet, a rail and motor vehicle crossing at the Second Narrows, completed in late 1925 by a private consortium. Promptly damned and rammed (sixteen separate accidents between 1925 and 1930) by harbour skippers, it was nonetheless a vital link in the burgeoning port. After the barge *Pacific Gatherer* hit the bridge on September 19, 1930 and took out the centre span, the Harbour Commissioners were reminded of its importance because the transshipment of railcars and freight across the inlet by barge now cost an additional $6,000 per month. When the original bridge company, now without toll revenues, went bankrupt in 1932, the Harbour Commissioners bought the severed span. On June 18, 1934, they reopened the bridge with a more ship friendly centre section. Rail service to the North Shore, as well as automobile and truck traffic, was reestablished.

The rail system grew, the Harbour Commission's tracks augmenting those of the CPR and being augmented on its own by the newly laid rails of the recently nationalized Grand Trunk and the Canadian Northern – now amalgamated as Canadian National. By the mid-1930s, as William McKee notes, Burrard Inlet was no longer where the rails met the sea – it was encircled by rails that tied its various waterfront

Traffic returns to North Vancouver on the Second Narrows Bridge on June 18, 1934 as trucks, railcars and automobiles cross the span.

facilities together, including the growing industrial centre of False Creek.

The former skid road port was now a major player. The decade of the 1920s and early 1930s saw Vancouver's central location as a way station between the major markets of Asia, North America and Europe become more and more apparent to the world's maritime industry. The port had not turned its back on its origins, with forest products still a very important commodity shipped out to Vancouver's biggest customers – the Atlantic Coast, Japan, the U.K., California, China and Australia (in that order), including pulp and paper, introduced in 1911 and 1913, respectively. Other goods leaving the port included canned salmon bound for China, salt herring for China and Japan, fish meal, fertilizer and fish oils, and lead, zinc and copper, which arrived at the port by rail before being shipped out to the U.K., Japan, Germany and France.

As the shipment of goods from Vancouver grew, so do did the influx of cargoes. The Port Annual for 1930 explained:

> The excellent and regular steamship line services between the BC Coast and Europe has created an increasing trade in importing via Vancouver the general manufactures required in Western Canada, and this tendency is increasing rapidly. Vancouver is becoming well established as a distributing centre

Two of the CPR's beautiful advertising posters from the great age of ocean travel. They date to 1927 and 1932. The "All Red Route" spanned the globe, and Vancouver was part of that worldwide system of British travel and trade.

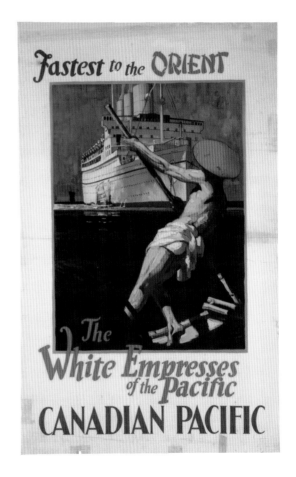

for British and European continental manufactured goods, as well as those of Oriental production, and also, of course, for the raw products such as tea, coffee, spices, etc., which reach these markets.

In 1930, 23,532 vessels arrived at Vancouver, and while most were regional or local coasters, 1,284 were oceangoing vessels. These numbers mean an average of 107 sailings per month, a far busier harbour than fifty years earlier.

Included in those sailings were the regular departures of the Union Steamships. The company had become more than just the commercial lifeline on the Inside Passage. The Union Steamships opened the coast up to the holiday seekers and tourists who were starting to flock into British Columbia. As well, the Union Steamships ferried weekend visitors and city folk to spots like Bowen Island, whose steamer landing became a well-loved port of call a short run from downtown Vancouver. Seeing the opportunity, local entrepreneur Harold Clay built up a fleet of motor launches that ran out of False Creek, Pender Harbour and Sunset Beach in Howe Sound. Named for the first vessel in Clay's fleet, the MS *Arrawac*, Arrawac Charters Line advertised its services as an opportunity to "See the BC Coast the Arrawac Way."

As Vancouver grew, so did the Fraser River ports, particularly New Westminster, which was, according to the Port Annual of 1930,

> the natural distributing centre for the whole Fraser Valley, one of the most fertile agricultural sections in the entire province. The principal industries include: lumbering (including all its allied products), car building, ship building, fishing, salmon and fruit canning, paper mills, chemical fertilizers, stock yards, meat packing, distilleries, foundry and machine shops, grain elevators, milling, cordage factory, etc.

Fraser River port authorities proudly and accurately advertised themselves as "Western Canada's Principal FRESH WATER Port."

But with growth came turmoil, particularly as the Depression of the "dirty thirties" affected the workers on the waterfront. Canadian exports dropped by half between 1929 and 1933, hitting Vancouver and New Westminster very hard. In Vancouver unemployment reached twenty-four percent. As shipyard worker Hec Smith reminisced, while he had a job in the yard, "there was no new work, everything was repairs, all dirty jobs, and we had to fight all the time to get dirty money and didn't always get it." Some of his fellow yard workers were on relief. If work came along – a rare thing since most yard workers at Burrard Dry Dock, the busiest yard, were only employed for three to four

The crew at Mercer Brothers' Star Shipyard at Queensborough, circa 1912. The family-owned firm remained in business until 1970, building fish boats and tugs. The original caption on this image reads "Fish boat building – Columbia River type – around 1912. In this group are, left to right: Jon Lugford; Harvey Mercer; Ed Mercer, owner of the yard; Jack McBeath; Ky Way and John Way; Art Mercer; and Gordon Mercer, sitting on the cross span."

THE MARINE BUILDING

One of Vancouver's great architectural masterpieces is the Marine Building at 355 Burrard Street. Built at the edge of the bluff and overlooking the harbour, the Marine Building was designed by architects McCarter, Nairne & Partners, to resemble a rocky promontory rising from the sea. The brainchild of local yacht club member and businessman J.W. "Joe" Hobbs, who allegedly made a fortune in rum-running, the Marine Building was one of Vancouver's first skyscrapers. It is also an Art Deco treasure, with its decorations celebrating aquatic life – sea snails, crabs, sea horses and a variety of fish – and the region's maritime history, including an entranceway tribute to Captain George Vancouver.

The building's construction at the height of the Great Depression and cost overruns of $1.1 million ruined Hobbs' fortune and he was forced to sell the building at a loss to the Guinness family, financiers of the Lions Gate Bridge and developers of West Vancouver's British Properties. The building was for many years the heart of Vancouver's maritime community, a headquarters and meeting place with panache all its own. Today, it hosts a variety of tenants, with some eight hundred people working in forty businesses, including the building's oldest tenant, Marine Printers, who have occupied their basement premises since the building opened on October 8, 1930.

The Marine Building, unencumbered by its modern neighbours, as it originally looked when built. Its architects conceived it as some great crag rising from the sea, clinging with sea flora and fauna, tinted in sea-green, touched with gold. The Art Deco masterpiece bankrupted its builder, but it remains a prominent and well-loved landmark at the foot of Burrard Street.

months out of the year, then the worker had to report the income, which was then deducted from his relief payments. Hec Smith recalled about two fellow workers, Joe Allen and Bill Murray: "Joe looked after his mother, and he and Bill . . . got two days' work and didn't report it. Joe was called up to court, and so was Murray, but Joe . . . was his mother's sole supporter, and he didn't get sent to jail. But Bill Murray got nine days in jail for not reporting two days' work, the first he had for weeks. That was how it was in the 1930s."

Times were also tough for the longshoremen, who saw their wages cut. In 1931, longshoremen made 83 cents an hour for dock work and 87 cents per hour for ship work. A bitter strike in October 1923 had nearly broken the International Longshoremens Association, with many longshoremen never returning to work on the docks after it, and while the harsh end to the dispute dampened enthusiasm for another strike for years, tensions rose during the Depression. In October 1934, a new labour contract between the Shipping Federation and the Longshoremens Union cut wages back to 76 cents an hour for dock work and 30 cents per hour for ship work. Several months later, a labour dispute in Powell River spilled over onto the Vancouver waterfront. The longshoremen refused to unload paper products shipped into Burrard Inlet from Powell River, and the Shipping Federation locked out the longshoremen.

On June 18, 1935, about a thousand longshoremen led by decorated war veteran Mickey O'Rourke marched on Ballantyne Pier to protest the lockout. The police waiting at the pier told the crowd to disperse. They fired tear gas and waded into the crowd. Twenty-eight longshoremen were hurt, and two dozen were thrown in jail in a melee the press termed "The Battle of Ballantyne." The events of that day were long remembered as "a black day for the Port of Vancouver," according to historian Norman Hacking, which "left a legacy of bitterness that persisted for many years thereafter." Rolf Knight, a longshoreman who grew up hearing tales of the "battle," recalls childhood talk about "Bloody Ballantyne."

The most powerful accounts were of how the RCMP had been brought in to smash the picket lines and how they [on horseback] had ridden down men who fled through the back streets and back alleys near the waterfront, pursuing their quarry even onto the porches and into surrounding houses. Yeah, we knew about that. But the story about police machine guns being set up at the dockyard gate seemed rather exaggerated. 'Not in Canada,' I thought, incorrectly.

The unrest of the thirties also saw the replacement of the old Harbour Commissioners and the end of local control of the ports. In 1933, unhappy with declining revenues, and suggestions of political interference and manipulation, the Dominion government commissioned a review. The resulting study recommended centralizing authority in Ottawa, and in March 1936, the government created a new National Harbours Board. Three commissioners in Ottawa answered to the Minister of Transport, and all revenues flowed east to the capital, rather than remaining in local hands. A port's revenues would be held and disbursed in Ottawa for the port's needs. In the new system, a local port manager would oversee affairs on the coast. Former port superintendent Ken Burns became Vancouver's first port manager, serving until 1947. While Burns worked hard for his port, and the new system "did much to clear up the financial morass into which some of the ports had fallen," according to Norman Hacking, Ottawa did not appoint a local advisory committee, and as a result "members of the Board were too often unaware of the distant needs of the Port of Vancouver," as well as the other Pacific Coast ports. The thirties, it seemed, were slated to end with the coast and its ports in the "economic doldrums." But war in Europe once again changed the destiny of the ports.

The RCMP stands by at the dock during the Depression-fuelled 1935 waterfront strike. The scene appears peaceful but soon would erupt into a bloody confrontation between longshoremen and police.

Local artist Jack Hardcastle (1881–1980) of Nanaimo made a living painting these popular souvenirs of the Union Steamship's vessels as passengers headed in and out of port; for many, no trip on a Union boat was complete without a Hardcastle. Shown here are some signature examples of his work.

Chapter Five

THE BOOM YEARS

1940–1959

IN 1939, CANADA HAD ENTERED its tenth year of economic hardship. The Great Depression still gripped the country. That decade of unrest and dislocation witnessed the rise of fascism in Germany and Italy, and a strong military-backed nationalist government in Japan. The aggression of those nations brought international tensions to a breaking point. When Nazi Germany invaded Poland on September 1, 1939, Great Britain declared war on Germany. Canada entered the war on September 10th. With war came an end to the depression, as had been the case in the First World War.

Once again the need for munitions, weapons and war material brought new jobs, and attacks by German U-Boats sent thousands of ships to the bottom, inspiring a new shipbuilding boom. The demand increased with the Pacific War against Japan after the Japanese attack on American, British and Dutch possessions and colonies on December 7, 1941.

The fortification of Vancouver harbour was one of the first signs of the war. During the First World War, four-inch (100 mm) naval guns hastily emplaced in Stanley Park above Siwash Rock, had "protected" the port, and now the old emplacement was rearmed, in as much haste in September 1939. The Royal Canadian Engineers built two new emplacements at the First Narrows and at Point Grey, first installing six-inch (150 mm) guns in temporary sand-bagged fortifications, and then building reinforced concrete batteries. At the Lions Gate, on the North Shore and west of the newly built Lions Gate Bridge, another emplacement, "Narrows North," guarded the harbour entrance with more guns and eight powerful searchlights to illuminate potential targets and keep on the look out for enemy submarines. One target for the soldiers at Narrows North was Prospect Point, across the water. After midnight they would "flick the beams" onto the Point and "with the

The Naval Examination Service's Hotchkiss gun at Point Grey, circa 1943. Used as a "stopping gun," the veteran six-pounder fired warning shots at vessels that did not heed the requirement to halt for inspection. On one occasion, a new freighter on a trial run was the unlucky recipient of a shot that went through her hull.

aid of binoculars, watch surprised lovers disentangle themselves to escape the all-revealing glare."

But the threat of enemy attack was real enough. The war with Japan brought Imperial Japanese Navy submarines to the coast, and in June 1942 submarine I-26 torpedoed the cargo ship *Fort Camosun* off Cape Flattery before heading north to shell Estevan Point Light. The attacks plunged the coast into a panic. In response to the war, the Union Steamship Company armoured their wheelhouses and painted their ships grey. After I-26's sortie, one of the Union fleet, the newly acquired (but long in the tooth) steamer *Camosun II*, was modified at Burrard Dry Dock to become a defensively-armed merchant ship – BC's first.

The choice was ironic. When news of I-26's attack on the freighter *Fort Camosun* reached Vancouver, many people assumed that it was the Union boat that had been lost. After its gun was installed and bridge reinforced with armour plate, *Camosun II* headed out for sea trials. The trials were attended by local naval officials "mostly with gold braid up to their sleeves," according to one crew member. Steaming out of the First Narrows and into the Strait, *Camosun* readied for action. The gun fired, and the light fixtures in the dining saloon crashed to the deck. The "old *Camosun*," said Union chronicler Art Twigg, "had to limp back into the shipyards for further modifications and reinforcing."

The war in the Pacific prodded local officials to take measures to guard the mouth of the Fraser, which the military had also fortified. At "Fort Steveston," two rapid-firing 18-pounder guns, according to the Army's "standing orders" for the region's coastal fortifications, were ready to "prevent vessels proceeding up the South Arm to New Westminster." In reality, the battery, built in October 1939, rested atop a "waterlogged dike" near the South Jetty in close proximity to Steveston's largely Japanese-Canadian population, both of which made the troops manning it uneasy. In fact, more than the troops were uneasy. Despite the fact that there were no cases of known espionage, sabotage or disloyalty, and that many of the "Japanese" were Canadian-born, fear and racism resulted in a military order to relocate them from the coast in response to the Japanese Navy's attack on Pearl Harbour.

Before the relocation, the first step was the rounding up of "Japanese fishing boats" two days after the Pearl Harbor attack. By the third week of December 1941, 1,182 boats had been confiscated, devastating the fishing fleet. Most of the boats seized by the government were sold for far less than their real value to white fishermen and went right back into business. Others were burned. The seizure of the boats was followed by the incarceration and forced removal of Japanese-Canadians from the coast beginning in February 1942, a terrible

action with profound consequences. Steveston, founded by ethnically Japanese fishermen and other immigrants with strong ties to the sea, and with a thriving Japanese community, was forever changed, as was the Powell Street area in Vancouver, another centre of Japanese settlement.

The panic over the Japanese also reflected a larger concern over the region's vulnerability to attack. Crammed with ships and full of shipyards bustling with wartime production, Burrard Inlet was a logical target for a surprise attack by a disguised merchant cruiser or an enemy submarine. With the coming of war, management of the Port of Vancouver passed to the Royal Canadian Navy, which estab-

lished a controlled zone inside English Bay where incoming ships would come under their scrutiny. When approaching the zone and the "examination line" that marked its western boundary, an incoming ship would have to slow, signal its identity with flags to two patrol craft (no private radio transmissions were allowed) and then proceed.

Unexpected or unadvertised ships were to anchor in an "examination anchorage" within range of Stanley Park's coast artillery to be inspected. Smaller craft – the regular users of the waterway – had recognition numbers painted on their sides to speed up their access and egress, not only at English Bay but also on the

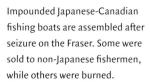
Impounded Japanese-Canadian fishing boats are assembled after seizure on the Fraser. Some were sold to non-Japanese fishermen, while others were burned.

Fraser, where Fort Steveston served as another examination station. The system was foolproof, or so it seemed.

Fog, mist, confusion and forgetfulness by some sailors, and human error, made for some interesting times on the water, especially since the gun batteries were under orders to open fire on ships that failed to obey the regulations. That usually meant a shot across the bows as a reminder of the rules. "A few fishermen and Sunday sailors learned this lesson the hard way," says military historian Peter Moogk. On September 13, 1942, a fish packer entering English Bay ignored signals to identify himself. As he approached the Lions Gate, the Narrows North battery, called into action, fired a single shot that stopped the packer. But the shell ricocheted off the water, skipping like a stone, and punched through the side of the steel cargo ship *Fort Rae*, on sea trials fresh out of Burrard Dry Dock. The shell tore through the ship just forward of the engine room and exited below the waterline, flooding the number-three hold. Amazingly, said the gun battery commander, "there was no alarm until they finished that testing run and turned to come into the harbour, at which time the hold was flooding and there was an obvious panic. They beached the hull inside the Lions Gate Bridge [and] I wasn't very popular with the ship's captain." *Fort Rae*, patched and pumped out, returned to the drydock for repairs and then headed off to war.

This ornamented gavel, carved with flourishes, two maple leaves, a folded anchor and braided rope, is surmounted by a beaver. The legend "Canadian Pacific Spans the World" is carved on one face. The striking surfaces of the gavel are encased in brass rings that are engraved "T.S.S. *Princess Marguerite*, Launched 26th May 1948," and "Fairfield Shipbuilding and Engineering Co. Ltd." Built by the Fairfield Company Ltd. of Glasgow, *Marguerite* joined her sister ship, *Princess Patricia*, on the BC coast as part of the Canadian Pacific Railway's coastal service. Starting in 1949, the two ships connected Victoria, Vancouver and Seattle. After a decade of service, the arrival of automobile ferries doomed the coastal service, and the CPR abandoned its regular run, but kept *Princess Marguerite* on a daily summer trip to Seattle until September 1974. Sold to British Columbia Steamships Ltd., the "Maggie," as the old steamer was affectionately known, continued in service until 1988. Sold next to Sweden's Stenna Lines, she remained in their fleet for only a year. Sold again, this time to become a restaurant in Singapore, Maggie finally ended up in the scrapper's yard in 1996. Her demise was greatly lamented in British Columbia.

Top: RCMP *St. Roch* returns home from Arctic service during the Second World War. In two epic voyages, 1940–1942 and 1944, the small wooden vessel became the second ship in history to traverse the notorious Northwest Passage. Now a National Historic Site, she is the centerpiece of the Vancouver Maritime Museum.

Bottom: *St. Roch's* port wheelhouse door key, from her original (1928) wheelhouse, demolished in 1944 when a new, larger deckhouse was built at Halifax's Dockyard for the second Northwest Passage voyage.

VANCOUVER MARITIME MUSEUM

Canada gained its first purpose-built maritime museum in 1958 when the City of Vancouver began construction of the "Centennial Maritime Museum" on the shores of English Bay. The genesis of the new museum, and its centrepiece, was the RCMP motor schooner

St. Roch, built at Burrard Dry Dock in 1928 and retired in 1951 after a long career. Sailing out of Vancouver to bring supplies and constables to Arctic outposts, St. Roch made world history in 1940–1942 when the dauntless Mountie schooner became the second ship ever to navigate the Northwest Passage, a feat repeated in 1944 when St. Roch returned to Vancouver from Halifax.

Opened to the public in June 1959, the museum's holdings have grown in its fifth decade to a multi-million-dollar collection of treasures that include the hand-drawn working charts from James Cook's third expedition of 1778, the flag flown by the famous British battlecruiser HMS Hood when she visited Vancouver in 1924, over two hundred marine paint-

ings, several hundred models, including a rare Napoleonic model of a man-of-war made of bone by French POWs, and tens of thousands of books, archives, charts and ephemera in the W.B. and M.H. Chung Library. The museum is also home to the deep-sea oceanographic research submersible PX-15 Ben Franklin, which made a famous thirty-one-day drift dive between Florida and Nova Scotia in 1969.

"Small on the outside, big on the inside," the museum and its Alcan Children's Maritime Discovery Centre is consistently rated a family favourite for tourists and local residents who come to learn more about the rich and diverse maritime history and ongoing marine saga of Canada's Pacific ports.

"Bone" model of the French man-of-war Le Vengeur d'Peuple, and a hand-tinted portrait of Empress of Asia bridge messenger Ernest MacLeod, who served aboard her during the First World War, just two of the treasures in the museum's vast collections.

Women shipyard workers at Burrard Dry Dock, circa 1944. The original photograph identified three of them. They are Evelyn Pearce (later McDonald), front row, third from the left, Lilian Matheson Rance, back row, second from the left, and Gertie Todd, back row, second from right.

The shipyards were the major maritime industry affected by the war. At the beginning of 1940, the principal shipyards in the region were Burrard Dry Dock, North Van Ship Repairs and BC Marine, all of which had survived the "dirty thirties" with difficulty. The war brought incredible change for them. In response to a government order for ships, Burrard Dry Dock expanded into two facilities, Burrard North and Burrard South, with some 11,000 workers. North Van employed nearly 6,000 workers. West Coast Shipbuilders opened up on False Creek and hired more than 5,000 workers. Gordon Farrington, who worked at Burrard during the war, recalled in 1977 that those who worked in the yards "came in the main from the small towns of British Columbia, or the Canadian prairies, and their work in those years is a proud confirmation of the adaptability of the Canadian people to meet strange conditions and adversity and to overcome them."

The workers in the yards also included women. Burrard Dry Dock, under the direction of Clarence Wallace, Alfred's heir, was the first shipyard in Canada to hire a significant number of women. One of them, twenty-two-year-old Doris McEwan, was Canada's first female welder. Jonnie Rankin first worked at Burrard as a sheet metal mechanic's helper and then at North Van Ship Repairs as a "passer girl." As she explained,

> A passer girl worked with the riveting crew – a riveter, bucker, and usually two passers. Her job was to catch the molten hot rivets in a cone-shaped bucket and feed them to a second passer who put them into the assigned holes. The bucker then jammed them into the holes and leaned on his riveting gun, while the riveter sealed them on the other side of the deck or shell or wherever you were working.

At the peak of wartime construction, the various yards employed 1,495 women, although by the summer of 1943 women shipyard workers had dropped to half that number. Alice Kruzik, a thirty-seven-year-old single mother with one son in the army

Pneumatic bolt tighteners follow a riveter at work at Burrard Dry Dock during the war.

and a fifteen-year-old son working at a sawmill, joined the workforce in February 1944 as a sweeper. After a while, she was approached and asked,

> 'How would I like to go below and earn some dirty money?' I said, 'Who the heck do you think I am? I came here to earn honest money and help the war effort.' 'Oh,' he said. 'I meant would you care to work in the tank in a confined space and earn about two hours' extra money?' I said I'd think about it. In the meantime, another woman got the job.

In addition to new construction, the yards were heavily involved in repairs and refit-

West Coast Shipbuilders launch a 10,000-ton ship on the shores of False Creek, June 11, 1944, one of 255 such vessels built at West Coast yards to support the war effort.

ting for Allied and neutral nations' ships. One major job involved the refitting of American aircraft carriers transferred to Great Britain in early 1944. As shipyard worker Gordon Farrington reminisced, the wiring in the ships "did not come up to the standards of the British Admiralty." Burrard Dry Dock did not have enough room to handle the carriers, and so a new yard was set up at the foot of McLean Avenue in Vancouver near the LaPointe Pier when "what had started out as a simple re-wiring job turned into a major overhaul" as each carrier was reinforced and braced against aerial bomb attack, a last-minute change in the contract. Jimmy Martinez, a Burrard superintendent, recalled that one of his first jobs at the yard was installing anti-aircraft guns on British ships heading home: "The captains of these ships hated to see me come around, because not only had I to install an anti-aircraft gun, but also I had to change some things on the ship. I often heard the captains say, 'Oh, here comes that little Spanish bastard. What's he going to have changed on my ship next?'"

By the end of the war in 1945, West Coast shipyards had launched 255 of Canada's 354 10,000-ton North Sands-type cargo ships. Of that, Burrard Dry Dock sent 111 of them down the ways. North Van, which had started the war as a ship repair and salvage yard, turned out 54 of the 10,000-tonners. West Coast Shipbuilders,

Bottom: The complex world of steel shipbuilding, North Vancouver, Second World War. Here workers are laying the deck plates for a 10,000-ton dry cargo ship in the summer of 1943. More than 20,000 shipyard workers helped fabricate, modify and repair hundreds of Allied merchant marine and naval vessels.

Right: Refitting the American aircraft carriers at Burrard Dry Dock; the flight deck is being extended.

WATERFRONT FIRES AND FIREBOATS

Vancouver gained its first fireboat in 1928 when J.H. Carlisle, named for the city's long serving fire chief, went into commission on False Creek. The 60-foot (20-metre) Carlisle, in operation until 1973, spent much of her career on the Creek, leaving the main part of the harbour largely unprotected. The agreement between the City and the False Creek property owners who financed the fireboat's construction required that the fireboat receive special permission from the mayor to leave the Creek.

J.H. Carlisle responded to occasional blazes in the harbour, including two notable fires outside the creek: the Pier D fire on July 27, 1938, and on March 6, 1945, when the freighter Green Hill Park, loaded with a wartime cargo of lumber, newsprint, tinplate, alcohol, chemicals and distress signals, exploded and burned at Pier B-C. A fire in the number-three hold of the ship set off what witnesses later said were four separate explosions just before noon, instantly killing two seamen and six longshoremen and seriously injuring twenty-five others. The blast racked the ship, shook buildings and shattered windows downtown. Harbour tugs pulled the burning ship free of the dock and toward the Lions Gate Bridge, where the tugs and J.H. Carlisle poured water into the burning holds for three days.

Vancouver Fireboat No. 2, an 87-foot (26-metre), 163-ton-boat, built at the Yarrows Yard in Victoria, joined J.H. Carlisle in 1951, but controversy over the City of Vancouver's insistence on keeping the boats in their jurisdiction led to demands for another, non-civic fireboat. The argument raged for decades, culminating when the retirement and sale of J.H. Carlisle in 1973 and the sale of Vancouver Fireboat No. 2 in 1989 left the waterfront without fireboat service for the first time in sixty years. That fact, and a disastrous fire that destroyed the Coast Guard's Kitsilano Base, spurred action. A federal-municipal partnership, including the Port, the City of Vancouver and neighbouring municipalities, agreed on a fleet of shared fast response fireboats in 1992, ending years of disagreement and recriminations. The new boats were designed by Vancouver's renowned Robert Allan Ltd., the port's oldest practicing firm of naval architects. With eight decades of experience, Allan has designed vessels for coastal, Arctic and Pacific service, as well as the workhorses of the waterfront – tugs, barges, patrol craft, fishing vessels, and fireboats.

Green Hill Park, still on fire, rests near Siwash Rock as the fireboat J.H. Carlisle fills the hold with seawater on March 6, 1945.

A crane lifts a boiler for installation into a 10,000-ton ship at West Coast Shipbuilders, circa 1944.

amenities ship, service personnel "could retreat and enjoy recreational facilities and a pub that served beer brewed on board from distilled seawater by a trained brewmaster. . . . It looked and tasted like a dark British brew, but being made from distilled water it was totally flat . . . so it was like drinking a beer-flavoured cough mixture, its main virtue being it was cold and wet."

The bustle of wartime shipbuilding led to a new name for Burrard Inlet, the "Clydeside" of the Pacific," more of a challenge to the Scottish shipbuilding centre than a tip of the hat. In addition to the shipyards, other industries boomed to supply the demand for ships. Dominion Bridge Co. and Western Bridge & Steel Fabricators produced the steel plate, while Vancouver Engineering Works and Progressive Engineering cast propellers and machinery. Westland Iron & Steel Foundries cast anchors and other fittings, and Vancouver Iron Works made boilers. The veteran Westminster Iron Works (founded in 1887) retooled for the war to make winches, wire rope hawsers and bulkhead hatches for the shipyards, while another New Westminster firm, Heaps Engineering, gas engine manufacturers, shifted to propulsion shafts and winches for North Sands ships.

By August 1943, a slowdown in production began as the war turned against Germany's U-Boats, and the need for large numbers of replacement hulls declined.

founded by a group of businessmen headed by Major G.A. Walkem, hired veteran shipbuilder W.D. McLaren to manage the yard and build 10,000-tonners. West Coast launched fifty-five of them from a yard built on the site of the former Coughlan & Sons yard on False Creek. BC's shipyards launched fifteen frigates, ten corvettes, twenty-two minesweepers and three landing ships for the Royal and Royal Canadian navies, the majority of them launched from Burrard and North Van.

West Coast Shipbuilders' last wartime contracts, issued in 1945, were for five maintenance ships for the Royal Navy and the conversion of the ship *Menestheus* from a minelayer to an amenities ship. As maritime historian S.C. Heal notes, aboard an

Orders for landing craft and ships for the invasion of Europe and the anticipated invasion of Japan occupied the various yards, but the end of the boom was in sight. In 1943, Burrard Dry Dock launched forty-two ships, which declined in 1944 to twenty-seven ships before dropping to seventeen launches in 1945. Burrard began lay-offs in August 1943 and continued through the end of the war as the number of launches declined. The same was true for the other yards. From a wartime high of 23,700 men and 1,495 women employed in BC's shipyards, employment dropped to 6,132 men and 159 women by 1946. But as shipbuilder T. Arthur McLaren later noted, while "there was no devastating economic slump in BC

A brass employee identification tag from Burrard Dry Dock.

shipbuilding after World War II, there was definitely a period of adjustment."

Large numbers of late-war-built merchant ships became available at much-reduced prices in 1946. The federal government sold many of the "Park" type ships to Canadian firms at half the cost of their construction to beef up the Canadian merchant marine. More than a dozen west coast companies, most based in Vancouver, bought the ships from the government, among them the Canadian-Australasian Line, Seaboard Shipping and the Western Canada Steamship Company. Oil companies like Imperial Oil, which had established its Ioco refinery near Port Moody before the war, bought seven wartime-built tankers. Refitting all of these ships for their peace-time uses occupied the local yards for the next few years. Burrard Dry Dock received additional work from the federal government for the coast's first diesel-powered cargo ship, and a lucrative contract from the French government for colliers. Burrard did well enough to buy out Yarrows, its Victoria competitor, in 1946, and North Van Ship Repairs in 1951.

The next decade saw slow but steady times for the shipbuilding industry, as the Navy modernized its fleet to meet the demands of the Cold War, and the rapid growth of pulp and paper mills on the coast led to the demand for more tugs and barges, built by the hundreds by Burrard and West Coast Shipbuilders. When West

The Union Steamships run to Bowen Island was a popular pre- and postwar excursion.

The daily steamers *Lady Alexandra* and *Lady Cecilia* made the hour-long trip for $1.40.

Coast closed in 1948, part of the yard was taken over by T. Arthur McLaren, who founded Allied Builders Ltd. (later Allied Shipbuilders) and started by building smaller steel vessels – tugs, fishing vessels and an ammunition lighter for the Navy.

While shipbuilding had assumed the lead role among the maritime industries of the region, the postwar years saw the resurgence of the ports. A dramatic decline in grain shipments had come with the war. In 1939, Vancouver had exported thirty-four million bushels, but by 1941 the shipments had dropped to six million bushels as the necessity of transporting war materiel took over the shipping lanes. But exports of grain and other "raw com-

modities" from BC picked up dramatically after the war as shipping lanes reopened to regular merchant traffic, and rebuilding Europe required the minerals, lumber and grain that Vancouver and the Fraser ports had to offer.

The first major change in the handling of cargoes came with unitization, or the synthesis of cargo, into standardized units that could be handled by mechanized or even automated equipment. Crates of goods, fruit, equipment, bales of wool and other items formerly loaded as bulk freight would go into containers that were then handled in one standardized manner – no matter what was inside them.

Over the centuries, ships evolved, from sail to steam, then to diesel, in larger sizes, to carry more cargo and to carry it faster. But for most of those years, except for the introduction of mechanical power for cranes and dockside vehicles, the basic method of handling most cargoes remained unchanged from ancient times. Block and tackle, nets and slings, and muscle power, along with the hook, were the standard tools for thousands of years. The difference between the hand- or horse-powered docks of a thousand years ago and the early 20th century was that mechanical power – steam "donkeys" and later, internal combustion engines – meant that larger loads from two to five tons, and then finally ten tons, could be placed in nets and slings, and then lifted into a ship.

Opposite: Handling cargo the old-fashioned, hard way. Longshoremen unload bales of raw silk from the freighter *Achilles* at Ballantyne Pier on May 2, 1929. The event was touted as the largest delivery of raw silk from the Orient ever shipped to Vancouver.

The grain freighters *Cellina* and *Benjamin Franklin* load at Burrard Grain Elevator in 1930.

But this was a slow and inefficient system. Hatches needed to be opened and closed, cargo carefully stowed. Ships were tied up in port for fifty to sixty percent of the year. It was also an expensive system, requiring large crews of workers, and long periods that still left ships idle for two-thirds of their time in port.

Unitization was first realized in the early 19th century. The Liverpool and Manchester Railway, beginning in 1830, used a standardized container developed for them by Pickfords, which in turn led to lift-on, lift-off containers that allowed easier loading, by slings, from railway cars to ships. But the practice was limited to coastal operations, and was largely confined to Great Britain.

The problem of efficiently and quickly handling large cargoes was thrust into the forefront during the Second World War. The United States, with its tremendous industrial output, was the world's arsenal, and billions of tons of matériel, munitions and equipment poured across the seas to the European, Pacific and Australasian theatres of war. American military planners conducted considerable research into unitization and developed small containers, but these cargoes were still handled by a bulk-break system. The postwar years highlighted the need to develop a new, more efficient means for moving cargo, but for several years the issue languished.

It took looking at the problem from a new perspective, in which ships became links in a global transportation system by land and sea in a way never before attempted. The key was the development of the standardized container that could be taken on and off trucks and railcars and placed onto ships built specifically to handle them.

The worldwide container revolution began with the Alaska-Yukon Pacific Railroad's *Clifford J. Rogers*. The 4,000-ton, 336-foot (101-metre) *Rogers*, laid down by Canadian Vickers at Montreal and delivered to Vancouver in November 1955, was the world's first expressly designed container ship. With it came six hundred fully insulated, seven-by-seven-by-eight-foot (11-cubic-metre) cube containers built locally. *Harbour and Shipping*, in its December 1955 issue, highlighted the arrival of this "radically-new container freight service":

> Her specially-designed cargo-handling equipment features steel containers of 5-ton capacity, insulated, heated or refrigerated as required. These self-contained units, assuring fixed temperatures from shipper to delivery point, eliminate spoilage of perishable goods. Handled by heavy duty fork lift trucks, the containers are loaded at the shipper's warehouse, and moved to the ship where they are locked in place in the hold by a system of removable steel bulk-heads. Arranged three deep and two abreast the entire length of the

Alistair Bell
Boats in winter, 1953

Fishing boats, tugs and barges are
the most commonly found working
craft on local waters.

Boats in Winter 13/15   Alistair Bell

A modern container ship. As container ships have grown, the need for modern dockside facilities to handle them has increased. The ports of Greater Vancouver have constantly upgraded to meet the need since the 1970s. In Vancouver, most container traffic is handled by Terminal Systems Inc. (TSI), which operates Deltaport and Vanterm on Burrard Inlet.

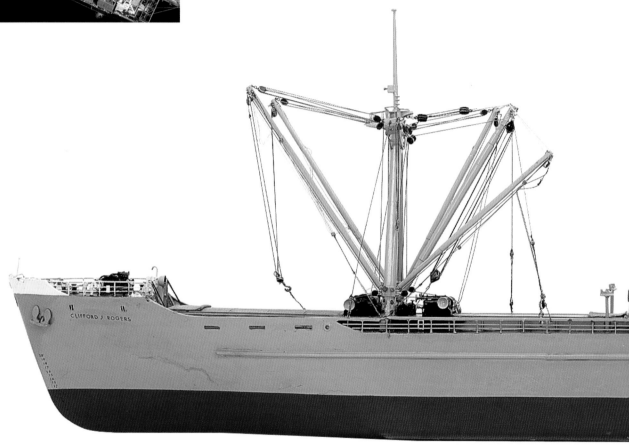

Model of *Clifford J. Rogers*. One of the treasures of the Vancouver Maritime Museum, the model depicts the world's first purposely built container ship. It joins one of the original containers, a life ring from the ship, and the ship's logbooks as some of the last relics of *Rogers*, which ended up sinking off Bermuda.

The tugboat *La Mite*, one of the small, hardworking tugs on the Fraser. Built in 1954, the wood-hulled, 34-foot long veteran of the river was sheathed in steel and renamed Gambier Chief in 1988.

hold, locked in place top and bottom to prevent lateral movement, the pilfer-proof, spoil-proof containers can't slide or topple . . . the containers . . . are de-signed to fit on railway flat cars and flat bed trailers.

Running between Vancouver and Skagway, Alaska, *Clifford J. Rogers* pioneered the con-tainer concept, a fact forgotten by many and usually not recognized in the history books published outside of Canada.

The postwar period also saw large conglomerates taking over what had once been hundreds of individual sawmills and consolidating and expanding operations. Transport of sawdust, wood chips and "hogfuel" by barge brought more work for tugs and increased traffic by water as tugs

towed logs to mills and then hauled out barges laden with the finished products and milling residues to pulp and paper mills up and down the coast and up river.

The North Fraser (the "North Arm" of the river) particularly benefited, as industry began a prolonged pull-out from Burrard Inlet and False Creek, now surrounded by urban development and increasingly under pressure from the City of Vancouver to vacate. The North Arm of the Fraser, sepa-rately administered as a port with its own commissioners since 1913, assumed great-er importance as a booming ground for the collection of large numbers of cut logs. It was also an easy trip to the variousmills that had sprung up the river's banks. Tug-boat skipper Howie Keast, reminiscing about taking logs up the North Arm, tells of long tows of thirty- to forty-section log booms heading in on a flood tide. "There would be two to four tugs on those tows, depending on the tide." The tugs would drop logs along the way, "then up to the top end and into the main river where they were delivered to various mills. It used to take sometimes two tides, but in the spring, when the freshet was on, it was hard going."

Adding to the difficulty were the sev-eral bridges on the Fraser that had to be threaded, a tough task with the tide flow-ing, or when the water was high. Captain Donald McPherson, who worked the Fraser on the tug *La Mite* in the 1950s, remembers taking medium-sized tugs "about 65 feet

Above: Many Union ships served as floating post offices, with mail delivery accepted on board. These are a few covers with ship-dated cancellation stamps.

Right: Bell from the Union Steamship *Catala*, the Company's premiere northern-run passenger and freight steamer, she was also known as the "Queen of the Union Fleet." Built in 1929, she ended service as the last Union Steamship in operation when the Company ceased running in January 1959.

THE LIONS GATE BRIDGE

Like the span across the Second Narrows, the bridge at the First Narrows was the subject of controversy and concern. Opposition to spanning the narrows began in 1892 and continued through the 1920s, spurred by efforts to keep a bridge or tunnel's thoroughfare from bisecting Stanley Park. Mariners, wary of obstacles, also argued against a bridge.

The development of the hillsides of West Vancouver by the Guinness brewing family and local entrepreneur A.J.T. Taylor in the early 1930s was the impetus for the bridge's construction. Despite the fact that both the province and the North Shore municipalities approved the bridge's construction in mid-1933, the City of Vancouver withheld its permission until Taylor agreed to pay for a plebiscite, which returned a 70.8 percent approval in December. Federal approval was not forthcoming until April 1936.

Work began on March 31, 1937, and continued through November 1938. On November 12, the bridge opened to pedestrians and two days later to vehicles. The 3,250-foot (975-metre) span cost $5.8 million to build. The clearances across the channel between its two towers and from the water to the bottom of the suspension was a uniform 200 feet (60 metres), which have remained navigable for most ships save modern aircraft carriers, although some larger ships wait for low tide to pass beneath the span.

The busy shipping that passes beneath the Lions Gate is surpassed by the traffic that uses the bridge. An estimated twenty-five million vehicles each year (averaging 70,000 vehicles each day) cross the bridge. Their wear and tear wore out the bridge by the late 1990s. After much deliberation, the Province of British Columbia, which bought the bridge from its developers in 1955, had it partially rebuilt between May 1999 and September 2002. In 2005, in recognition of its significance, the Historic Sites and Monuments Board of Canada designated the Lions Gate Bridge as a National Historic Site.

The Stanley Park approach to the Lions Gate Bridge in the early days. The cast concrete lions, the work of sculptor Charles Marega, were installed a year after the bridge opened. Modern commuters who cross the bridge daily might wish for a quiet day like this.

A workaday reminder of a dangerous trade, this caulk boot with its spikes lining the sole was essential gear for the hazardous job of working on log rafts.

long with 600 horsepower" to move barges loaded with wood chips and hogfuel up and down the river "as far away as Mission to the tie-ups off Point Grey where the outside tugs would come, drop off their empty barges, pick up the loaded barges and take them to the pulp mills. Then we'd take the empties back up the river, two or three at a time, and drop them at different mills."

The towboat industry, heavily involved in the transportation of log rafts and barge tows, also grew during the decade – and over the next twenty years reorganized as mergers, takeovers and buyouts changed the face of towing on the coast. These were "hurley-burley days of . . . highly charged entrepreneurial activity" in towing which saw the rise of several smaller towing com-

panies. Some of them were family concerns and owner-operated tugs like Straits Bros. on the North Arm, the father and son team of Harry and Jack Bruno, who towed booms for Canadian Western Lumber, and William Beckman and his son Amos, whose "fleet" consisted of the 40-foot (12.2-metre) *VB* and the 30-foot (9.1-metre), 30-horsepower *Tugaway*.

Another new company, founded by towboat operator Bob Cosulich and his business partner Harry Burt, was the River Towing Company. Their fleet of small tugs started with *Red Fir No.1*. The "Red Firs" were 35-foot (10.7-metre) shallow-draft vessels that opened up the upper Fraser to log tows. When Harry Burt left the company, his place was taken up by Cosulich's son Cecil, and later, another son, Norman, joined the business. That business thrived and became Rivtow, which in time was purchased and renamed Smit Marine, now the preeminent towing firm on the Fraser.

THE CHANGES ON THE FRASER were mirrored in Vancouver. In May 1953, the Port reported that Vancouver, "Canada's gateway to the Pacific . . . only now is flexing its commercial muscles and looking toward new economic horizons that bid fair to increase the importance of city and port." While the much-publicized hopes of Vancouver's mayor Fred J. Hume to fill in the rest of False Creek for development did not take place, the 1950s saw port construction that began to transform the waterfront. In 1956, construction of Centennial Pier commenced west of Ballantyne. When completed in 1958, the new five-million-dollar facility included four dockside cranes, covered storage for 200,664 square feet (18 580 square metres) of cargo and outdoor storage space for another 250,830 square feet (23 255 square metres) of cargo. The new site covered several football fields and at the time seemed large. As trade grew, however, it would soon seem too small.

The Second Narrows, whose bridges had been the source of controversy, condemnation and a number of marine accidents, saw additional incidents in the 1950s. In 1956, the provincial government began construction of a new, larger bridge at the narrows. The new bridge lived up to the site's reputation on June 17, 1958, when a 375-foot (125-metre) anchor span and a 282-foot (85-metre) deck span collapsed into the inlet. The damages reached $3.5 million and twenty-four men died – eighteen ironworkers and engineers who fell with the spans and died that day, five who subsequently died of their injuries, and a diver killed while searching for bodies. The bridge would not be completed until August 1960, when it opened as the longest bridge in western Canada.

By the end of the decade, the waterfront had seen not only a growth in development and a modernization of the Port of Vancouver, but also a return to busy deep sea and coastal trade. But that did not extend to passenger service. The Union Steamships did not survive the decade, ending service in January 1959 when the veteran steamer *Catala* docked for the last time. The decline of many smaller communities on the coast as the forest and fishing industries also changed with the times, closing mills and canneries, had played a part in the end of the Union ships and an older way of life.

But it was also a time of increased urbanization and the growth of Greater Vancouver and its ports. A University of British Columbia study noted "in the relatively short period of seventy-five years, Greater Vancouver has grown from a sawmill town at the end of the transcontinental railway to a metropolis of over 600,000 persons and an international port which in 1959 handled twelve million tons of goods in coastal and foreign markets." The port now had seventeen berths for deep-sea ships and three for coasters, and could handle 576,000 square feet (51 840 square metres) of cargo and nearly ten million bushels of grain. The time had now come for Vancouver and its surrounding ports to enter the global stage like never before.

Tugs mill about the scene after the fatal collapse of the Second Narrows Bridge (now Ironworkers Memorial Bridge) killed 18 workers on June 17, 1958.

Chapter Six

RISE OF THE PORTS

1960 to the present THE LAST DECADES OF THE 20TH CENTURY and the beginning of the 21st have been turbulent times. These years of rapid change have witnessed increasing globalization and growing awareness of new challenges – environmental, social, and political – that have changed the way we perceive the world. New technologies have radically restructured the way we work and live. For some, to paraphrase Dickens, they have been the best of times, while for others, they have been the worst of times. New technologies have replaced traditional means of work, and cost people their jobs. New global partnerships have, as has always been the case, brought new opportunities for trade. The new global market has also introduced new realities.

The Fraser and fishing as it was, circa 1870. With two canoes pulled up on a beach, a fisherman harvests the river in the ancient and traditional manner. The salmon is drying on the racks. Within a few decades, the rise of canneries and fleets of fishing boats changed the old ways, forever.

The Asian recession of the late 20th century cut trade and jobs, and a softwood lumber dispute with the United States badly hurt the timber industry and those who ship BC's forest products by sea and river. New social awareness and changing attitudes introduced environmental protection programs, consultation and compromise, and compensation for past injustices of seized lands and lost opportunities with the First Nations. A growing number of women joined the waterfront workforce, many in what once was considered "a man's job."

These have also been years of disruption – not just because of change but because of disputes and clashes over different priorities. Municipalities increasingly value waterfront lands not for port development or a seemingly now dreaded "industry," but

for waterfront condominiums and green space. Vancouver as a place hugs the water, with no land access to the north, and for tears with its access south limited. There was also not much access east except by the river, and so the City was truly a maritime entity, dependent on the water for its growth and sense of self. That changed in the late 20th century. Corporations and government seek to downsize to maximize profit, but at a very human cost. Dramatic declines in salmon stocks have ravaged the fishing industry and led to bitter controversy over allegations of government mismanagement, unfair advantage granted to First Nations fishery workers, new technologies and techniques resulting in over-fishing. Often these controversies have led to no consensus, only bitter debate.

It is perhaps an overstatement, then, to say that over the span of decades from the 1960s to the first years of the new millennium, the Port of Vancouver and its counterparts on the Fraser witnessed the most dramatic changes they had ever seen. True, they became global gateways and dominant players in North American and world shipping as their waterfronts transformed, in part owing to the changing nature of trade, and in part owing to the postwar growth of the region's communities. Yet they did so in an always shifting, and not easily navigated, landscape of politics and economics that profoundly changed the way they and their partners in industry, as well as those who labour on and around the water, now work.

Improvements in cargo handling facilities in the Port of Vancouver came about thanks to persistent lobbying by Port Manager Captain B.D.L."Barney" Johnson and his staff, and by local shipping firms that had protested to Ottawa for years that Vancouver's harbour facilities were outdated and required renovation. Johnson's tenure from 1955 to 1969 was marked, as had been that of his predecessors, by rule of the Port from a bureaucracy in Ottawa, far removed from the coast. The National Harbours Board sent its commissioners, most of them political patronage appointments from the east, for a brief annual visit "to have a look at Canada's premier Pacific Port." Not surprisingly, little understanding of the local issues and few substantive results, according to some who worked in the Port in those years, ever followed these visits.

Nonetheless, Barney Johnson, a man with formidable energy, managed to find ways to get things done incrementally, never fighting the big battle but slowly and carefully winning the smaller fights – an addition here, a renovation there – to improve his port. He persistently argued and lobbied, particularly when, much to his dismay, his annual budget surpluses went east "to shore up the ailing port of Montreal." Johnson, known colloquially around town as "Young Barney," was, like his father

"Old Barney," a retired naval officer and a forceful mariner. The father and son Johnsons were perhaps the most dominant and influential maritime personalities in the Greater Vancouver area – no mean feat for an industry dominated by powerful personalities both in the boardrooms and on the docks and decks. The younger Johnson persisted with a patient if not stubborn determination that won him the respect of the waterfront community.

The 1960s commenced with Vancouver Port's expansion of the old LaPointe Pier, renamed Centennial Pier, and the construction of new bulk cargo facilities throughout the length of Burrard Inlet. By 1963, the Port of Vancouver was already Canada's leading port in terms of tonnage, thanks to its massive exports of bulk commodities. Vancouver Wharves at the First Narrows and Pacific Coast Bulk Terminal at Port Moody were developed to handle the burgeoning trade in potash from newly developed mines in Saskatchewan, coal from Alberta and eastern British Columbia, and sulphur, the natural by-product of BC's and Alberta's oil and gas wells. Vancouver Wharves later expanded its operation to accommodate other bulk commodities like copper concentrate and sulphur, pulp and paper, and packaged lumber. The National Harbours Board constructed Neptune Terminals, a dry bulk cargo facility, located near the site of S.P. Moody's long-closed mill in North Vancouver, to handle coal,

Model-builder Doug Allen has built a remarkable set of models that depict the evolution of fishing boats that have worked the Fraser River and the coast of BC for the last century.

Bottom: *B.C.P. 103* – Built circa 1910, this BC Packers one or two man rowboat was one of many craft towed out in groups to a likely fishing spot by a tender.

Top: *Game Over* – This highly efficient aluminum hulled boat represents the latest technology and design, circa 1980.

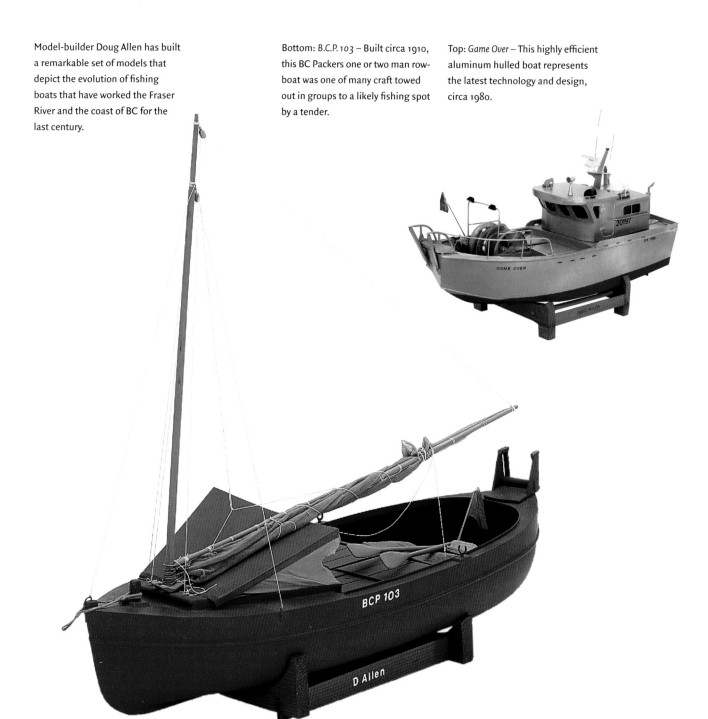

Top left: *Terra Nova* – One of the earliest powered boats, with a one cylinder, four to six horsepower engine, circa 1920.

Top right: *St. Mongo No.11* – Powered by an Easthope engine, she carried the first powered drum, circa 1930.

Bottom left: *Orea No.1* – This ground line fishing boat worked primarily for halibut, circa 1947.

Bottom right: *San Juan* – This large gillnetter, equipped with the best modern technology of the day and nets of up to 3,600 feet (1 100 metres) in length, circa 1955.

Harbour tugs maneuver a bulk
freighter into dock at Neptune Bulk
Terminal, next to Saskatchewan
Wheat Pool in North Vancouver.

Through these facilities the bounty
of western Canada's mines and
wheatfields reaches the world.

potash, specialty grains, chemical fertilizers, canola oil and phosphate rock. When it opened in 1960, Neptune was hailed as the largest multiproduct bulk terminal in North America. The new terminal could ship 4,400 tons of coal an hour, fed by a continuous loop system of railcars.

Seaboard Terminal, another new bulk facility at the mouth of Lynn Creek in North Vancouver, was built up from dredge spoils between 1968 and 1971. When it opened, Seaboard became the world's largest forest products terminal, shipping the commodities harvested from British Columbia's forests to an international market.

The 1960s also saw a renewed expansion of the grain trade, thanks to demand from a growing Asian market. A resurgent Japan, recovering from the devastation of the Second World War, had reemerged as a major trading partner. So, too, did China. The failure of US-China relations following the Communist revolution excluded China as an American market and trading partner. Canada and its Pacific ports benefited from Washington and Beijing's mutual hostility. By 1961, exports to China and Japan made Vancouver the world's largest grain shipping centre. New grain handling facilities sprang up on the waterfront, exemplified by the 1966 construction of the Saskatchewan Wheat Pool Elevator on the North Shore. Construction doubled the capacity of the Alberta Wheat Pool, as well. A sign of the new facilities'

capacity to efficiently and quickly ship grain came in 1975, when a then-world-record single grain cargo of 4.8 million bushels of wheat and rapeseed (used to make canola oil) was loaded aboard the Bangladesh-bound tanker *Amoco Cairo*.

The spate of waterfront construction continued through the mid-1970s on both Burrard Inlet and the Fraser River. But Burrard Inlet was reaching its capacity, and port expansion was testing the patience of politicians who saw little value in industrial land, and sought higher tax returns from redeveloped waterfronts full of residential units. Municipal planners, responding both to the wishes of the politicians and desires to transform the face of their waterfronts and communities, did not support massive redevelopment of port lands. This was particularly the case in Vancouver, where the industrial/port city of the preceding decades – the source of the city's birth and growth – was now seen as an embarrassment by some who wished to build a post-industrial cosmopolis on the shores of the inlet at the expense of a working waterfront.

Even as quiet – and occasionally public – battles raged over the development of the waterfront, a study analyzing Burrard Inlet's ability to handle an anticipated near-tripling of the annual tonnage of dry bulk exports it would handle in the next two decades discovered that a protracted fight to build up the waterfront by more landfill and new facilities was a losing proposition. It was "apparent that even with extensive improvement, the existing harbour could not benefit fully," according to a University of British Columbia commissioned study. The answer lay in moving out of Burrard Inlet. The readiest site for expansion was the delta of the Fraser, and so in November 1966 Vancouver Port, in a brilliant strategic move, had Ottawa sanction its expansion out of the inlet "to include all tidal waters south of the Burrard Inlet to the 49th Parallel." While North Fraser and Fraser River Ports still ruled the banks and waters of the Fraser and its arms, Vancouver Port stretched past the river's entrances to the American border, and close to it, settled on a site for a massive redevelopment at Roberts Bank.

The demand for coal by Japan's resurgent steel industry provided the opportunity to take the first step in achieving the vision of filling in the mudflat of Roberts Bank to build a new "super port" well away from the pressures and problems of an urban setting. The impetus was a long-term contract between Nippon Kokan K.K. and Kaiser Resources to deliver millions of tonnes of coal to Japan. The Roberts Bank loading bulk terminal, a massive filling project with rail and highway access, arose on landfill just south of the South Arm of the Fraser in the lee of the point in 1970.

Built by the government but leased to Westshore Terminals, a Kaiser subsidiary,

the Roberts Bank terminal was to be the first step of a megaproject that would have filled in the intervening five-kilometres between the terminal and the shore for a surrounding industrial park. Until those mudflats were filled (which ultimately never happened for a variety of reasons ranging from environmental, political and plain old economics), a narrow causeway linked the terminal to the shore. Across it a steady stream of railcars delivered coal to waiting ships. The new terminal prospered as the production of coal skyrocketed in the decade that followed, thanks to new mines coming into production.

The creation of the new areas for processing Vancouver's bulk cargo trade was matched by the development of facilities for handling containers that were now dominating the world's ports. Even though the concept of containerization had been pioneered on the North Shore terminal of the White Pass & Yukon with *Clifford J. Rogers* in 1955, pleas to the National Harbours Board for container cranes were ignored for years, much to Barney Johnson and his industrial partners' frustration. As Ottawa fiddled, "the rival port of Seattle was able to take a commanding lead in the North Pacific container business," infuriating Vancouver Port officials.

Nonetheless, in 1966, Barney Johnson commented, either in publicly good-natured optimism or good old-fashioned stubbornness, that "containerization is

The awe-inspiring scale of modern maritime commerce and tourism that flows through Vancouver is captured in this view of of an immense cruise ship, carrying thousands of passengers on the Alaska run, and a supersized transporter, stacked high with a rainbow of containers, distributing products from throughout North America to the Asia Pacific and beyond. Here, APL *Kennedy*, which can load between 4,000 and 5,000 containers, is docked at Centerm.

TYMAC

Among the busiest vessels in Vancouver harbour are those owned by Tymac. Working 365 days a year, around the clock, the Tymac fleet of launches, barges, workboat, water tanker and tugs keeps busy delivering supplies, water and crews to ships and hauling away shipboard garbage, as well as serving as a water taxi service and as pilot launches.

Founded in 1930, Tymac has been in business for two-thirds of the working life of the Port of Vancouver. Alexander "Sandy" McKenzie, superintendent of B.C. Marine, left the yard after the slowdown in shipbuilding at end of the First World War. Taking a job with water taxi entrepreneur

Warren Hastings, McKenzie decided to go into business on his own and began building his first vessel in his backyard. A young English shipwright, Sam Tyson, assisted McKenzie and did all the "tiddly work." It was a slow project, as McKenzie could only work on the boat in his off hours, but in 1930 the 35-foot long craft, christened *Tymac* (for Tyson and McKenzie) was finally completed.

Powered by a St. Lawrence, the marine version of a Fordson tractor engine, *Tymac* was a jack-of-all-trades: handling ship's mooring lines for ten dollars a job, working as a water taxi, hauling lumber from Howe Sound

and Indian Arm, and acting as a charter boat. As Liz Bennett noted in a 1980 history of Tymac in Harbour & Shipping, "rates were low and hours long."

In 1938, McKenzie built a sister ship, the launch *Tymac No. 2*. Fitted with the first Chrysler Crown marine engine and keel cooler on the coast, *Tymac No. 2* was kept busy during the Second World War working under the control of the Navy. Tymac Launch Service worked a gradually expanding trade, carrying freight and crews to ships at anchor on English Bay. McKenzie added *Tymac No. 3* to the fleet in 1946 to handle the increasing work.

Alexander "Sandy" Mckenzie founder of Tymac.

Tymac No. 2 "rises on the ways" in McKenzie's backyard, 1938.

McKenzie brought his son Dave into the business as soon as the lad could help handle lines, and in time Dave McKenzie took over the responsibility for his father's company. In 1972, the delivery of a new vessel, *Kimsquit Belle*, bought to become *Tymac No. 4*, introduced the McKenzies to Clem Phillipson, the marine superintendent of the Southern Division of the Prince Rupert Fisherman's Cooperative Association. Phillipson handled the sale of the vessel, and soon found himself negotiating with the McKenzies, who had decided to sell the business and thought

Phillipson was the right buyer. On January 1, 1973, Clem Phillipson took over Tymac.

Like the McKenzies, Phillipson ran it as a family business. In 1974, Clem's son Jim and Jim's wife Cathie bought into Tymac, and in 1988 they purchased the remaining fifty percent of the company after Clem retired. Under the Phillipson family, Tymac prospered along with the growing port. The fleet grew in the 1970s, added a shop scow for on-the-water maintenance, a water tanker and a freight launch. In 1979, Tymac acquired the assets of Hattco

Marine Services Ltd., their chief competitor, adding more vessels, and moved to a twenty-four-hour dispatch service.

The company continues to grow and diversify. Innovative, hard working and entrepreneurial, the Phillipsons have weathered economic slowdowns in the Port, the redevelopment of the waterfront and the resultant two moves of the company's offices and dockside facilities since the 1980s, and the need to become their own vessel repair facility with the closure of Menchions, the last shipyard on Burrard Inlet.

Builder's model of *Tymac No. 2* she survives to this day, as does the model.

Bottom left: A Gantry Crane unloading containers from a vessel at Fraser Surrey Docks.
Bottom right: Pulp from coastal and interior mills is exported overseas to make an array of paper products. *Star Grindanger*, docked at Lynnterm, takes on pulp for Asia. Pulp is fragile and must be loaded under retractable overhead covers. On-board gantry cranes handle up to 68 tonnes per lift.

just around the corner . . . and we are making preparations for it." Those preparations were, in keeping with the limited resources Barney and the Port had at their disposal, not major, but they were a significant improvement. The Port added a new container berth to Centennial Pier. When Berth No. 6 opened for business on June 1, 1970 it provided the venue for Vancouver's first regularly scheduled container service, which commenced quickly when the ship *Golden Arrow* pulled up to Centennial Pier.

It was an important step. By 1969, when Barney Johnson retired, he had won the day for his port – Vancouver now outstripped Montreal in terms of tonnage handled. Barney's successors learned from

his example and followed his incremental approach to win over their distant overlords and wrestle funding from Ottawa for new facilities. In 1971, Acting Port Manager W. Duncan warned that "the number of containers being handled at the Centennial Pier terminal is already greater than we anticipated." To answer the need, in 1973 the Port's patience and persistence paid off with Ottawa's approval for construction of two new facilities built on the foreshore of the inlet. Vanterm, a container, roll-on-roll-off and general cargo berth adjacent to Centennial Pier, and Lynnterm, a deep-sea cargo facility and adjacent industrial park on the North Shore, both opened in 1975.

The new facilities came just in time.

The '70s was an era of rapidly expanding ship sizes – supertankers were one aspect of a phenomenon that saw larger bulk carriers and container ships, a fact commented on by longshoreman Bill Chestnut in 1975: "Ships are getting so big – this used to be a three-berth dock and now it is a two-berth dock."

The changes in ships and the advent of containers altered not only the face of the waterfront, but also the way ships were loaded. The major change was an increase in mechanization.

Mechanization, necessary to handle the increased trade volumes, dramatically affected the conditions of employment for waterfront workers. The number of long-shoremen and stevedores required shrank with mechanization, and as one worker explained, "it brought the specialists, Crane Operators, Ship Loader Operators, Fork Lift and Straddle Carrier Operators, etc." The change was not universally accepted, and many jobs were lost to machines, a theme played out in other industries and jobs throughout the world at the same time. It was, and remains, one of the waterfront's major labour issues and a source of contention and compromise.

Bill "Spider" Smith, a longshoreman who started working on the docks in 1936 at age sixteen, commented in 1975 on the changes brought by mechanization:

> When I started with Empire Stevedoring, and that wasn't too many years ago, we had a fleet of about 8 dock lift trucks. . . . Now we have about 250. We have them all the way up to 80,000 pounds that handle both containers and steel. . . . We usually take five full shifts on a full container ship. Our net average is 19 containers an hour. That's in and out.

In the past, a general cargo ship, unloading the older bulk break way, had taken up to 150 men both on the ship and the dock as opposed to only a handful of men nowadays.

In 1985, longshoreman Robin Sutherland described the unloading of a lumber ship:

MV *Palma*, a roll-on-roll-off (ro-ro) vessel docked at Fraser Wharves, which is one of Canada's only two West Coast auto terminals – together handling all Asian cars entering Canada. A ro-ro is a ship designed for cargo that rolls on and off its decks. The ro-ro's plain box shape disguises its contents – as many as 6,000 new cars ready to hit the road. More Asian import cars are shipped through Fraser River Port than any other port in Canada.

The 1920s were a busy time on the Fraser. Here, workers load lumber onto ships at New Westminster's Pacific Coast Terminals. The New Westminster waterfront was in transition; the terminal has been extended an additional 200 feet (60.96 metres) to make way for more railroad track, roads and wharves. A boom in lumber exports from local mills had sparked a demand for more modern, rail-linked facilities.

Opposite: With the help of a couple of longshoremen, steel pipes are being unloaded at Fraser Surrey Docks.

In addition to the foremen for ship and for hatch unloading, there were slingmen, who sling or unsling the lumber, and one forklift driver inside the hatch. On deck will be one utility man to act as a go-between for those on deck and for those in the hatch, and one crane or winch operator and his signal man, who trade duties every few hours. On the dock will also be two slingmen. Thus eight longshoremen are required for each hatch, a far cry from the twenty or thirty required before mechanization.

Greater specialization among workers made necessary by mechanization raised a resultant expectation of higher rates of

pay and additional benefits, an issue that dominated the dialogue on the waterfront between the employers and unions.

Tremendous changes on the Fraser mirrored those in the Port of Vancouver. The 1950s ended with the construction of a new highway south through the Lower Mainland to connect with the U.S. border. The newly opened Massey Tunnel beneath Deas Island and the Fraser's waters linked the Lower Mainland with this highway, and with the government's new Tsawwassen terminal of the BC Ferry Corporation, provincially owned since 1958, located near Point Roberts. This new transportation route offered a dramatic challenge to the ports on the Fraser, which had to adapt or die.

The New Westminster Harbour Commissioners lacked the ability to develop modern facilities and maintain a competitive edge because they could not control all the river's industrial sites, many of which fell under different jurisdictions. The provincial government had developed Tilbury Island as an industrial site, and Richmond had developed others, none of which followed into the Port's coffers. Port business was also undercut by the new freeway to the US border, a move that Fraser Port historians maintain only exacerbated the port's frustration over lost opportunities and revenues because it opened up the BC market to trucks crossing the border loaded with containers that were

PACIFIC RIM STEVEDORING SWL 50 MT. 06/99

An unprecedented 4,936 automobiles were unloaded from MOL's new generation Pure Car Carrier M.V. *Liberty Ace* at Fraser Wharves Ltd. on March 26–27, 2005 – setting a record for cars discharged from a single ship at the Fraser River Port. The record was later broken by M.V. *Cougar Ace*, which unloaded 5214 cars on May 4, 2005. Fraser River Port is Canada's largest mover of Asian import automobiles, importing 436,931 vehicles in 2004.

Opposite: The revitalized New Westminster waterfront, part of the gateway port administered by the Fraser River Port Authority. The modern facilities of Fraser Surrey docks are in the foreground. In the background is Annacis Island.

pouring into American ports, notably Seattle, that had jumped ahead of the government-hampered Canadian ports to expand and to compete with southern British Columbia's ports.

While they fumed and planned for expansion to meet the competition from the United States, in 1962, the Harbour Commissioners nonetheless summarized the previous decade as one of "impressive growth," as some forty major industries expanded or built new plants: "Sawmills . . . today have new industrial neighbors making paint and varnish, laminated beams, steel shapes, aluminum extrusions and a host of other products." The Port proudly advertised the availability of deep-sea industrial sites on the "Pacific seaway of the future," while listing its existing facilities:

Commissioners' Wharf in New Westminster, Pacific Coast Terminals and Pacific Elevators. But behind the record of proud achievement was the realization that more was needed to better compete with both Vancouver and the American ports on Puget Sound. One of the first obstacles to tackle was not Ottawa, but local squabbling and competition.

The Harbour Commissioners and the Fraser's municipal governments faced a choice, as historians Jacqueline Gresko and Richard Howard put it: "get together and fight for a port with local input, or they could let the commission and port die. They got together." In 1964, under the Federal Harbour Commissions Act, a new regional Fraser River Harbour Commission was born and with the neighbouring cities took up the task of "regional seaway development and provision of up-to-date facilities for shipping."

The next two decades brought the consolidation of new general cargo and container facilities at the Fraser Surrey docks, opposite New Westminster. Another major development was created on Annacis Island. In 1972, the Harbour Commission began preparing the island for use as a deep-sea port facility, primarily to accommodate the burgeoning imports of Japanese-manufactured automobiles, arriving aboard roll-on-roll-off vessels that ferried the cars on enclosed decks across the Pacific. Nissan Motors pioneered the way,

Bertram C. Binning
Boats and Flags, 1948

Prairie native Bertram Binning compulsively incorporated his passion for the ocean around Vancouver into increasingly abstract, nautically themed paintings throughout the 1940s and 50s, even on a mural wall at the entry to his house.

During the years 1971 to 1973, Allied Shipbuilders yard in North Vancouver built five 191-foot-long (58-metres-long) offshore supply vessels: *Lady Joyce, Lady Lisbeth,* *Lady Vivien, Lady Jean and Lady Alexandra.* They were intended for service in the North Sea, delivering fuel, cement, water, drilling pipe and related materials to offshore drilling rigs. Below, within two hours after the launch of the *Lady Joyce,* the bow was fitted to the sister ship *Lady Lisbeth.*

From their two-cylinder gas engines to the heavier four-cycle marine engines they pioneered in 1918 for the Fraser River fishery fleet, the products of the Easthope brothers were the best small-boat marine engines to be had. Easthope Marine Engines was founded in 1900 by Vincent Easthope and his father Ernest, who had emigrated from England to Canada with his family in 1889. When Vincent died at age 23, his brother Ernie joined the firm. They sold Easthope Marine Engines, but the firm failed in 1910. By 1914, however, George Easthope and his younger brother Percy had bought back the old name and restarted the business, which lasted until 1968. Easthopes were used in fishing boats, motor yachts and a variety of craft in British Columbia and nearby Washington State.

followed by other manufacturers, who joined forces to create Annacis Auto Terminals in 1977. Within a decade, Annacis Island and the auto terminal handled all Japanese car imports into Canada except for Toyota Motors, which opened its own facility just beyond Deas Island. Linked by rail as well as by water, Annacis in time grew to handle imported BMWs, Mercedes, Volvos, Volkswagens, Renaults and Jaguars brought by train cars.

While the industrial face of the waterfront flourished with the development of new dockside facilities, hard times loomed ahead for the area's shipbuilding industry. The dreams of urban planners and politicians to clear the waterfront of industry began to push out long-standing businesses, notably Coal Harbour's many

boat and shipyards. They also focussed on clearing False Creek of its many industries. In 1967, Vancouver's last major shipyard, T. Arthur McLaren's Allied Shipbuilders, moved from False Creek to North Vancouver in close proximity to the Wallace family's Burrard Dry Dock. Both yards kept busy, building and repairing vessels for a variety of clients, including BC Ferries. Government contracts for both the Navy and the Coast Guard, as well as the bread and butter of coastal tugs, barges and fishing boats, occupied the ways at Allied as well as nearby Burrard Dry Dock for the next few decades.

Burrard Dry Dock, sold by the Wallace Family in 1972, passed into corporate hands, and for a while persisted, building ferries for the B.C. Ferries Corporation, trailer ferries for Canadian Pacific and icebreakers for the Coast Guard. But as business declined and government subsidies dropped off, in December 1992 the yard, known as Versatile Pacific since 1985, finally closed. With many of its buildings demolished and the wind whipping off the inlet to create dust-devils and mournfully howl through the last standing structures like the ghosts of old dockworkers, at the beginning of the 21st century the site located near Londsdale Quay in North Vancouver awaited redevelopment into a residential and retail complex.

Another landmark, Matsumoto Shipyards – begun in 1950 by returning interned

Japanese Ichijuro "Phillip" and son Isumo "Sam" Matsumoto, later joined by his son Ken – had built wooden and steel fishing boats and yachts and pioneered aluminum construction in British Columbia. Like the old Burrard Dry Dock, Matsumoto Shipyard did not survive in the lean years that began in the 1980s, and it closed in 1988. But the yard was not demolished, instead being transformed by the ever-resourceful McLarens into Allied Shipbuilders' Dollarton Ship Yard.

Allied survives, as does Vancouver Shipyards, relocated from Coal Harbour by Seaspan and now part of the Washington Marine Group of Companies. Vancouver Shipyards, while building and repairing

vessels for others, provides Seaspan (and now WMG's large amalgamated fleet of Cates and other companies) with new tugs, barges and repairs. One notable project in the 1990s, branching out into large-scale aluminum vessel construction, saw the yard's major participation in the construction of the "Fast Cat" aluminum ferries for the British Columbia government.

Controversial still, the Fast Cats, while magnificent vessels, were costly and ill-suited for the short runs on which the government placed them. The need to slow while entering and leaving dock, as their speed sent out bow waves that nearby waterfront property owners claimed were damaging docks and eroding their shorelines, meant

Coal Harbour, 1921. The former working waterfront was transformed by urban redevelopment starting in the 1960s.

COAL HARBOUR

the fast ferries design brought little advantage on their routes.

Highly politicized and criticized, the Fast Cats were adeptly characterized in a May 1999 attack on the New Democratic Party government of Glen Clark by the British Columbia's Leader of the Opposition, Gordon Campbell: "This Premier and this government have . . . soaked taxpayers for $445 million for fast ferry Ferraris that are stuck in a garage and won't work." A year later, government minister Joy McPhail, in answer to further questions from the Opposition, was forced to admit that the ferries would be sold:

Yes, we are selling them. However, there is also a recognition that the fast ferries are well built. That is not under question by any expert in the field. Yes, it is true that they are not suitable for this market and that they shouldn't have been built for these routes.

Withdrawn from service, the Fast Cats were sold, ironically, to the Washington Marine Group, who adroitly acquired very valuable commodities for resale as a result of what many saw as a classic example of ill-advised government interference that led to cost overruns, public condemnation and their ultimate dispersal at fire-sale prices.

The Washington Marine Group's ship-building operations in the early 21st century

Opposite: Although most ship construction is now the work of yards in cheaper labour nations, the Port of Vancouver maintains facilities to repair, refit and recondition some of the larger oceangoing vessels.

Here, the *Jade Forest* is undergoing repair at Vancouver and Panamax drydocks after running aground and suffering hull damage.

Bow of the designer's half hull for the freight and passenger steamer *Northland Prince*, built at Burrard Versatile Shipyards in 1963. The model shows the layout for plating the hull.

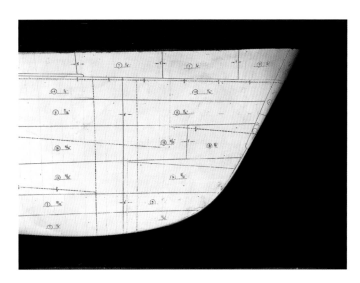

included outsourcing construction to Shanghai, where the company's Seaspan (Cyprus) Limited has built a series of barges, including four 212′ x 52′6″ (64 x 16 metres) deck barges for wood chip transport. After construction, the barges, double-stacked and launched in a single unit, were towed across the Pacific for completion at Vancouver Shipyard for final details and painting before entering service. Part of WMG's Seaspan Offshore Group, the shipbuilding venture, managed out of Vancouver along with the company's overseas container line and ship management services, is part of a shift toward the global market and away from reliance on what has been a less than stable local and regional market.

The fast ferry controversy continues to dog BC shipbuilding, and in 2004, a highly controversial government decision, this time by a new British Columbia government, turned to foreign shipbuilders to construct three new ferries for BC Ferries for half a billion dollars. Neither Allied nor Vancouver Shipyard gave up, submitting bids in early 2005 for a new 125-vehicle ferry for the Bowen Island run. It was a typically determined decision for both yards.

In the case of Allied, the firm, still a family-owned business, employs now-deceased Arthur McLaren's three sons, who continue their father's tradition. Allied has built more than 250 vessels, including seven ferries for British Columbia, and persists in a tough business by emphasizing ship repair. The last vessel built in the yard was the 50-foot-long (15-metres-long) harbour patrol vessel *Takaya*, built in 2001. *Takaya*, designed by Robert Allan Ltd., in business themselves since 1930, was another joint effort of Allied and Allan, who built a wide range of working craft. Allied also created a Western Machine and Coast Engineering Division to manufacture hydraulic tow pin/hook units, and to both manufacture and repair shafting and stern gear equipment, which occupies the company's workforce and keeps the firm in business despite the decline of the industry. Pragmatic and determined, the McLaren family has persisted for more than five decades as one of Greater Vancouver's maritime institution.

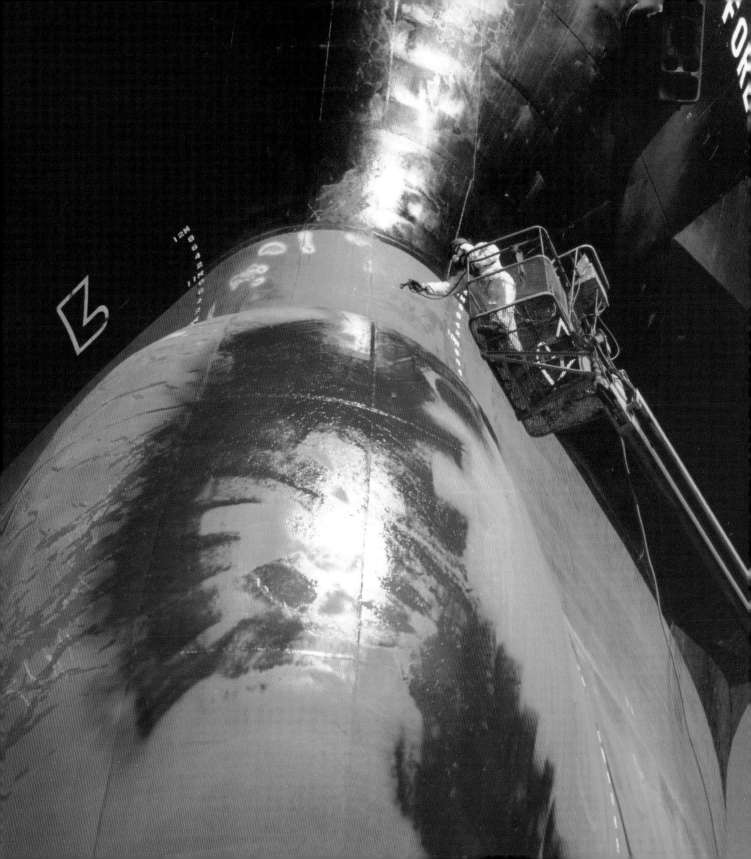

THE OLDEST AND LARGEST

When Harold Jones chartered his first tow with his steam tug *On Time* in 1898, Vancouver was a young city still growing out of its lumber mill beginnings. As the port city grew, so did Jones's business. In 1905, he had the tug *Le Roi* built for him, following her with *La Belle, La Mars* and *La Reine*. Jones also gave his son, Harold Jones, Jr., a tug of his own, *Rosina K.*

In 1925, the younger Jones and his sister Ruth used the tug *Atta Boy* to start up the Vancouver Tug Boat Company. In 1928, they added *La Reine* and hired Arthur Lindsay as general manager. Under Lindsay, the company won a contract with the forestry firm of Wood and English to tow pulpwood chips 250 miles (400 kilometres) from Vancouver Island to Port Townsend, Washington. It was 1932 and the heart of the Depression, and the contract was the bread and butter the new company needed. After that, according to historian Ken Drushka, they "never looked back."

Vancouver Tug grew in 1956 when it bought Dolmage Towing. Harold Jones died that year. Arthur Lindsay took the reins, three years later, aided by Jim Stewart.

Under Lindsay and Stewart, the company continued to grow with additional mergers and acquisitions, absorbing Vancouver Barge Transportation (1962), Pacific Tanker Company (1964) and Western Tug & Barge (1965).

In 1965, the company purchased the old Domtar property in North Vancouver and built its new headquarters, a shipyard and moorage for its fleet of twenty-six tugs and 155 barges. With the yard, which it expanded in 1969, the company was able to branch out into building its own tugs and barges. That same year, the Dillingham Corporation bought the Vancouver Tug Boat Company, and in 1970, merged it with Island Tug & Barge, then owned by another international corporation, Genstar. The new Vanisle Tug and Barge, now completely owned by Genstar, became Seaspan International in 1973. A year later Seaspan was an integrated deep sea and coastal transportation company with a fleet of forty tugs, two self-propelled railcar barges and 223 towed barges, making it Canada's largest tug and barge fleet.

In 1977, Seaspan's owners acquired another rival, the Gulf of Georgia Towing Company. Seaspan passed to new foreign owners in 1986, who in turn sold the company to a Vancouver group of investors. By the early 1990s, the company employed over a thousand people and operated a fleet of forty-five tugs and over 250 barges, ranging from Mexico to Alaska. In 1996, Seaspan entered a new era when the Washington Corporation purchased it along with veteran Burrard Inlet firm C.H. Cates & Sons Ltd., Kingcombe Navigation and Vancouver Shipyards, among others, and formed the Washington Marine Group of Companies. Seaspan has weathered many challenges and survives into the 21st century as a locally-based, international company with a long and distinguished history.

Washington Marine Group's Cates tugs maneuver the freighter *Stellar Fortune* into dock. These harbour workhorses have a long and distinguished career of assisting ships and working the waterfront.

Sign from the Menchions shipyard, a symbol of the vanished Coal Harbour waterfront. The redevelopment of the Vancouver waterfront has swallowed up the past of the working port in this area. Recalled now only by old timers and a street name, Menchions was a Vancouver and West Coast institution founded by William R. Menchions, famous Canadian boatbuilder from Bay Robert, Newfoundland. Arriving in Vancouver around 1896, Menchions worked as a carpenter, then as a boatbuilder for the Easthope Brothers. In 1912 he started his own yard. In 1941, the firm became W.R. Menchions Co. Ltd. One of the Port's leading boatyards, it survived W.R.'s death in 1947. When Menchions closed in 1990, they were the last wooden shipyard in Coal Harbour.

The old waterfront passed into memory over these decades. Rolf Knight, reminiscing in 1980, noted that much of the older industrial infrastructure had gone the way of the wrecker's ball, "even the old grain elevators, which seemed as solid and massive as mountains . . . . The glowering mass of the Rogers' Sugar refinery . . . still stands little altered, a salient reminder that life and work along the earlier waterfront was far from rosy."

Politically-spurred redevelopment on the waterfront began to displace industry throughout the waterfront. Coal Harbour, home to a number of ship and boat yards, began to gentrify in the 1960s, a move signaled when the new Bayshore Inn opened in 1961. The decade also witnessed the

dramatic transformation of False Creek. By 1963, only three sawmills were left on the creek, and in 1967, Allied Shipbuilders relocated to North Vancouver.

In 1968, Vancouver City Council voted to remove False Creek's industrial designation to spur other industries and companies to relocate. That left Granville Island as a largely unoccupied site, ripe for some form of redevelopment. While some in the City saw it as an area for a mix of housing and other taxpaying occupants, one federal politician did not. The late Ron Basford, Member of Parliament and a senior cabinet minister, had the island transferred from the National Harbours Board to the Canadian Mortgage and Housing Corporation to redevelop the island as a "people place" that preserved the island's industrial look and heritage. In 1973 the federal government helped form the Granville Island Trust. Sparked by these actions, by 1978 a renovated Granville Island with restaurants, shops, artist and craft studios, and a public market (which opened in 1979), was the first major step in the transformation of False Creek. Only one industry remains today, Ocean Cement, whose barges connect its Fraser and False Creek facilities, and whose trucks daily dispatch their loads to the region's many building projects.

False Creek's face changed with the construction of residential housing by Granville island, and then even more in

Vancouver's False Creek was the industrial heart of the city and a working port that grew up with the town, starting in the late 19th century. While boatyards turned out larger vessels, smaller vessels served the same role as modern delivery trucks, taking advantage of rail connections and the creek itself as a means of transportation. Here the work force of Coughlan's Shipyard stand in front of the ways and sheds of the shipyard on May 9, 1918, the tail end of the World War I shipbuilding boom. Where modern highrise condominiums and park lands now dominate the shores, shops like Vancouver Granite Company (bottom left), shown here in 1923, plied their trade. The Vancouver Lumber Company's log rafts fill the creek (bottom right) in this 1928 view from the site of the Cambie Street Bridge.

Once the shoreside economic hub of Vancouver, False Creek was home to an array of industries. Starting with the creation of Granville Island Market in the 1970s, and accelerated by the transformation required for hosting the 1986 International Transportation Exposition, EXPO 86, False Creek became a much studied and envied international example of inspired urban redevelopment.

With the removal of industry, salmon have returned to its waters, and dinner-plate sized turtles nest on its banks.

1986 as Vancouver hosted the world on its shores at Expo 86, a spectacular exposition that brought visitors from around the world for a year-long celebration. Expo 86 highlighted the tremendous change in False Creek, and the city's residents began to refocus on the creek as a centrepiece, not the "shit creek" sobriquet it had earned in its industrial heyday. Expo was a major incentive for investment not just in the event but in the city, furthering the change into a cosmopolis instead of a port town, although ironically enough one of the highlights of Expo was a "boom boat ballet" by small boats used in the lumber industry to manoeuvre log booms on the water. The show was magnificent, as many attendees recall.

Choreographed by Viktoria Langton,

four boom boats utilized their ability to swirl, swerve and spiral (essential skills in wrangling logs) to create a memorable show Langton vividly described as a performance where they "swayed and waltzed and danced to the Nutcracker Suite, conga and Latin music, and 'The Ride of the Valkyries'." While magnificent, the boom boats in False Creek in 1986 were by then only tokens of what had once been the dominant activity on those waters.

The end of Expo and the demolition and moving of many of its structures left a few landmarks – the Plaza of Nations and Science World – now surrounded by new highrise residential developments and a waterfront ringed by marinas full of recreational vessels ranging from sailing dinghies to high-end power yachts.

Changes on the Fraser meant demolition of older facilities in New Westminster in the 1980s, and the opening up of the city's riverfront for new, non-industrial development which included New Westminster Quay and its waterfront public market. Environmental changes to improve the river's quality, including the restoration of shoreline habitat for the benefit of both birds and fish, the bundling of logs to reduce snags and deadheads, the dramatic reduction of sawmill waste in the river, all were hallmarks of programs initiated by the Fraser River and North Fraser ports.

One sign of changing times was the retirement of the venerable snagboat, Sam-

son V, in 1981. Fraser Port donated it to become a floating maritime museum, a role it popularly and proudly fulfils after two decades in its new life. The Quay itself was the decade's largest redevelopment project and a great success after its August 1985 opening. It now also hosts the Fraser River Discovery Centre, which interprets the river, emphasizing "the economic, natural historic, aesthetic and spiritual worth of the Fraser River and its basin."

The trend toward more public access brought new facilities to Burrard Inlet and English Bay waterfronts even as they were in the throes of an industrial transformation as the port modernized and expanded. The new developments included a seawall path ringing Stanley Park, a new waterfront park (known to the locals as "Crab Park") near Centennial Terminal, and a new passenger ferry service after proposals for a third bridge or tunnel across the inlet were rejected. Seabus service commenced in June 1977 as the catamaran vessels *Burrard Beaver* and *Burrard Otter* began crossings of the inlet from Vancouver to Lonsdale Quay, another waterfront beautification project, adjacent to Cates Towing and Burrard Dry Dock in North Vancouver.

But the most striking physical change was the dramatic reconfiguration of the old Pier B-C as Canada Place, a landmark cruise ship terminal, convention and exhibition centre, World Trade Centre and hotel complex, which opened in December 1985, with the adjacent Pan Pacific Hotel opening early in 1986. The Vancouver Port Corporation began operating Canada Place as a cruise ship facility on April 28, 1986, and in that Expo year the new terminal handled 185 cruise ship sailings as well as hosting a variety of events on the pier and on the nearby water.

The decades after 1960 saw phenomenal success in the cruise industry. Alaskan sailings had declined following the closure of Union Steamships. But in 1960, the modern Alaska cruise ship industry was born, with chartered ships, among them the CPR's Princesses, which would ultimately inspire the famous Princess Cruises. Voyages to the "Norway of America" grew in popularity as cruise ship sailings along the Inside Passage increased from thirty-eight to 348 sailings per year, and Alaska became the third most popular cruising destination in the world.

Each year now, more than a million revenue passengers pass through Vancouver on their way to travel the magnificent waters of the Inside Passage aboard vessels of the leading cruise lines of the world, all members of the North West Cruise Ship Association. At the dawn of the 21st century their member lines were Carnival Cruise Lines, Celebrity Cruises, Crystal Cruises, Holland America, Norwegian Cruise Line, Princess Cruises, Royal Caribbean International, World Explorer Cruises, and Radisson Seven Seas Cruises.

NORTH TO ALASKA

Tourism to Alaska began to boom after the Second World War. By the early 1960s a variety of hotels, gift shops and other amenities had sprung up, especially in Skagway. To reach Skagway, visitors had to drive the wartime-built Alaska Highway up through British Columbia, and take the White Pass and Yukon train from Whitehorse or Carcross in Yukon Territory. Floatplane flights from Juneau on Alaska Airlines were another way.

The time-honoured means to reach Alaska and Juneau was, however, by ship. The run to Alaska, busy in the early century thanks to the gold discoveries, had remained an active commercial link between Vancouver, Victoria and Seattle, but by the 1960s only a handful of vessels served the needs of tourists. They were the CPR steamers *Princess Kathleen* and *Princess Louise*, which had entered service in the 1950s, the Canadian

INTERNATIONAL CODE P.Y.U. (BON VOYAGE)

Top: Cabin 51 on the Alaska cruise line *Yukon Star.*
Left: This printed passenger list is for an early Princess Line cruise to Alaska; the ships were smaller then. Today, the list of passengers is kept on computer as modern cruise ships can accommodate thousands of guests.

National steamer *Prince George*, which had worked the coast since 1948, and Chuck West's Alaska Cruise Line, which operated the steamers *Glacier Queen* and *Yukon Star*. West, a former bush pilot, had founded a tour company in 1946 to introduce tourists to Alaska's wilderness and scenic wonders, and in the summer of 1957 he helped inaugurate a new era of cruising when he founded the Alaska Cruise Line. *Glacier Queen* and *Yukon Star* were former Royal Navy corvettes converted into cruise ships by Union Steamships, which as it approached the end of its corporate life on the coast sold them to West. The demand for more ships ultimately inspired the birth of the Alaska Marine Highway System in 1960, and the resulting addition of new ferries beginning in 1963, as well as the birth of more cruise ships and the creation of what remains today as one of the world's most popular cruises: the Alaska cruise up the Inside Passage. West added a new vessel, *Polar Star*, to his line. The changing and expanding industry boomed, but the aging *Glacier Queen* and *Yukon Star* ended up sold in Vancouver, their homeport. Harbour Ferries agreed to purchase them to serve as floating hotels at Granite Falls, at the head of Howe Sound, but the death of Harbour Ferries' president in 1971 terminated the deal and the two remained laid up; three years later, *Yukon Star* was towed to Seattle and broken up for scrap. *Princess Patricia*, which replaced *Princess Louise* on the Vancouver to Skagway and Juneau run in 1963, was built by the Fairfield Company Ltd. of Glasgow. She was launched on October 6, 1948 to join her sister ship, *Princess Marguerite* (2) on the BC coast as part of the Canadian Pacific Railway's coastal service. They would be the last two CPR *Princesses* to work on the Pacific coast. Starting in 1949, the two ships connected Victoria, Vancouver and Seattle. After a decade of service, the arrival of automobile ferries

These brochures from the last decade of Union Steamships' life on the coast illustrate the Company's new shift to tourism and the Inside Passage run to Alaska as the number of stops on the British Columbia coast diminished.

doomed the coastal service, and the CPR ended its regular run, but kept *Princess Marguerite* on a daily summer trip to Seattle. *Princess Patricia*, refitted as a cruise ship with additional accommodations added to her car decks in 1963, ran to Alaska in her new configuration that summer, a pattern she continued each season through the next two decades. When the CPR was not using *Princess Patricia* they chartered her to Stan McDonald of Seattle. McDonald used her for his first two seasons (1965/66 and 1966/67) between Los Angeles and Acapulco before branching out to other vessels. He named his new line Princess Cruises after *Princess Patricia*. Retired in 1983, *Princess Pat* ended her days as a floating hotel ship on the Fraser during Expo 86, and was then sold abroad to work as a ferry, but instead was broken up.

Top: This souvenir pennant, sold aboard the ship, is from the veteran CPR steamer *Princess Patricia*. It is a small but vibrant reminder of the *Princess* ships and their link to Alaska, as well as the birth of the Alaska cruise ship industry. Bottom: The Carnival Cruise Line's *Carnival Spirit* docks alongside Canada Place. The 963-foot long, 88,500-ton vessel carries 2,124 guests as she makes her regular departures from Vancouver to cruise up the Inside Passage to Glacier Bay, Alaska.

Workers sort raw logs being loaded aboard a container vessel bound for Japan in the Port of Vancouver, October 1999. Environmentalists and some in the forest industry maintain that the export of raw logs means lost jobs in local mills and small businesses.

Their ships, some of the largest, most technologically advanced, comfortable, luxurious and safe vessels in the world, attract thousands of observers as they sail in and out of Vancouver.

Many of them sail out of Canada Place, which expanded in the new millennium to accommodate more ships and passengers. This expansion followed a 1991 decision to rebuild nearby Ballantyne Pier in anticipation of a near-doubling of vessel traffic by 2010. On May 12, 1995, Ballantyne reopened after an upgrade to serve cruise ships as well as forest products. Equipped with high-tech mobile passenger gangways, the redeveloped pier was heralded by its clients as an "efficient cruise ship

terminal with the simultaneous operation of year-round general cargo handling, making Ballantyne a forerunner in such multi-purpose facilities."

The last decades of the 20th century, particularly beginning in the 1970s, were the years in which women returned to work the waters and waterfront as a significant part of the workforce. While always part of life and work on the water, the postwar years and the social climate of the time had discouraged women from working on the water, as Sue Milligan, whose father had a log booming contract in Vanguard Bay, discovered in 1972 when she and partner Bob Harris tried to get a job on the project. Sue's father hired Bob right away, but he refused to take his daughter because "girls don't do that sort of work." He eventually relented, as did society in general as gender gradually ceased to be an issue.

Gina Johansen, who has worked the waters for most of her life, starting as the daughter of a fisherman, once commented that in the fishing industry the women who work in it insist on being called "fishermen." As Gina explains, "it's a job title, not a gender issue." Another mariner, Tymac Launch skipper Donna Chisholm, who joined Tymac in 1989, commented in 1995, "after six years, I'm just one of the guys now."

In 1995, journalist/author Vickie Jensen chronicled Sue, Donna and many other

Sue Milligan exemplifies the independent spirit and hard work of the region's female fishermen. Sue taught herself how to fish. Owner and operator of the fishing boat *Henry Bay* for sixteen years, Sue fished for rock cod in the waters off Vancouver Island. She says, "As soon as I saw the *Henry Bay*, I knew it was the boat I wanted. She was built in 1948, same year as me, and she drew about the same amount of water, five-foot three, so I bought her."

women's stories in *Saltwater Women at Work*, a landmark publication that interviewed and told the story of 110 women who worked these waters as skippers, deckhands, fishermen, engineers – in short, every type of job in what had once falsely been described as a man's world. Among their ranks were owners and operators, and one of the most unusual personalities in the marine industry of the region, Lucille Johnstone.

Joining Rivtow in 1945 with what was described as a "Girl Friday" job, Lucille branched out into dispatcher, purchasing agent, and with determination (she regularly worked twelve-hour days until well into her seventies) Lucille climbed the company ladder. It was the best thing that could have happened to the company. Taking an accounting degree in 1951, Johnstone used her skills to build Rivtow, then saddled by debt and with little cash, into a major company. Her forty-five-year tenure saw Johnstone rise to Chief Operating Officer and President of the Company, and when she retired, Rivtow (now Smit Marine Canada) was a $250 million-a-year conglomerate with more than 1500 employees.

Even in retirement, the indefatigable Johnstone was a hardworking volunteer, actively involved in the community as well as CEO of St. John Ambulance and founding President of the Fraser River Discovery Centre, one of her favourite projects. When she died on December 31, 2004 at the age of eighty, Lucille Johnstone, whose honours included the Order of British Columbia and the Order of Canada, was not just seen by many as the most distinguished woman in the marine industry, but one of the best, male or female, in the history of the industry on this coast.

The 1990s were important years for the ports of Greater Vancouver. By 1989, the Port of Vancouver had become the largest in North America in terms of tonnage of imports and exports. Nearly ninety percent of that tonnage was in bulk, mostly coal and coke, followed by grain and sulphur. Vancouver's exports now included oil sent to Burrard Inlet by the Trans Mountain Pipe Line. From Trans Mountain's terminal and

PILOTS

In British Columbia there are two groups of pilots: the Fraser River Pilots and the BC Coast Pilots. The Fraser River Pilots are responsible for piloting any ships on the Fraser River. The BC Coast Pilots are responsible for piloting all the ships on the remaining areas of the coast from the Washington State border to the Alaska border, including all of the areas around Vancouver Island and the Queen Charlotte Islands. There are currently eight Fraser River Pilots and 106 BC Coast Pilots who work for the Pacific Pilotage Authority, a crown corporation formed in 1972.

The modern-day pilots follow a long tradition that began in Victoria, Nanaimo and on the Fraser in the mid-19th century. In 1920, the first pilot organization, the British Columbia Pilotage Association, formed, followed by others that in 1929 became the British Columbia Pilotage Association. The 1950s and '60s saw a growth in the number of pilots as the maritime industry expanded. In 1963, because of changes in government regulations and the pilot districts, the Corporation of British Columbia Coast Pilots formed, and in 1973 the present-day company, BC Coast Pilots Ltd., came into being.

Burrard Inlet, the heart of the Port of Vancouver, more than a century after its inauguration as Canada's gateway to the Pacific Rim.

A Canadian Pacific locomotive pulls out of Roberts Bank after delivering railcars full of coal to the busy terminal. In the background, the container cranes of Deltaport rise above the coal. Deltaport is operated by Terminal Systems Inc. (TSI), the Port of Vancouver's largest container terminal operator. Deltaport's Super Post-Panamax gantries and docks accommodate the largest container ships in the world. The development of Roberts Bank and Deltaport greatly expanded the capacity of the Port of Vancouver. The intermodal transportation evident in this image, both in containers and coal, fulfils the original promise of the region when Vancouver was first developed after the Canadian Pacific Railway's selection of it as the terminus of the transcontinental railway and the trans-Pacific steamers. More than a century later, the rails still meet the sea for the benefit of Canada.

Imperial Oil's Ioco facility, oil for domestic use was shipped in small coastal tankers and tug and barge combos, while larger tankers shipped oil to Asia.

In early 1997, the Vancouver Port Authority opened Deltaport, at Roberts Bank. Built to handle the largest modern container ships, with four container gantry cranes, it is capable of handling ships in two container berths. All was coordinated by a computerized operating system and an on-dock intermodal facility with a capacity for two double-stacked trains and direct access to the CN and CP transcontinental rail systems. The addition of Deltaport to Vancouver's existing facilities doubled Vancouver's container capacity. By 2001, thanks to Deltaport, Vancouver was handling 1.1 million foreign containers.

In 2000, the Port of Vancouver's terminals and docks transshipped nearly 77 million tonnes of cargo, worth more than $30 billion, shipping to and from ninety international trading partners, firmly establishing Vancouver as Canada's largest and most diversified port. Fraser River Port, now Canada's second largest port, became an international link in its own right and the centre of a diversified intermodal network. At the same time, Greater Vancouver had grown into a major, multicultural metropolitan area of 2,041,399 persons.

North Fraser Port, meanwhile, retained its strong position as a working river port. A major transportation link and home to the forest and construction and supply industry, it also had become one of the continent's largest booming grounds, storing a third of the lumber cut from British Columbia's forests. The North Arm had also become a redeveloping industrial and urban riverfront with a strong emphasis on environmental issues, as the North Fraser Port Authority, like its neighbouring ports, worked to reclaim habitat.

The Fraser River, in the late 20th century, had at last achieved its potential as a great aquatic highway. By 1997, a fleet of over 200 tugs and 800 barges, the essential domestic link to the markets of coastal British Columbia, laden with forest products, wood chips, pulp and paper, as well as petroleum, sand, gravel and cement, were running out of the river as well as

Two new 55 metre (180 foot) tall "Panamax-size" container cranes destined for Fraser Surrey Docks were carried majestically up the Fraser River, towering high above the deck of the heavy lift ship *Dock Express 10*, on April 1, 2005. The semi-submersible ship lowered itself deeper into the river to get the massive cranes under Alex Fraser Bridge and several high-voltage electrical lines. Fraser Surrey Docks is the container and general cargo terminal at Fraser River Port, and is a key logistics hub in the Greater Vancouver Gateway. Fraser River Port is Canada's second busiest port based on total cargo volume.

"Siwash Rock". $\frac{20}{60}$ *E.J. Hughes /37.*

Edward J. Hughes
Siwash Rock, 1937

Known to the Squamish as S'i'lix, this prominent landmark dominates the harbour entrance. According to E. Pauline Johnson (Tekahionwake), who related the ancient Squamish story in her book *Legends of Vancouver*, Siwash Rock is a transformed man, a young chief and father who defied the spirits to swim and be pure as his wife bore his first child. His love of his child and his faith were rewarded with immortality, as were his family, who are the rocks that stand beside him.

Burrard Inlet. Canada's two largest tug and barge operators, Seaspan International and Smit Marine, and smaller operators were moving millions of tonnes of domestic cargo each year.

In March 1999, the Canada Marine Act, which made Vancouver, Fraser River and North Fraser more autonomous Port Authorities, came into force, in recognition of the ports' strong international links, as well as their importance to the provincial and local economies. The frustrations of absentee landlord control were now a thing of the past, with locally appointed boards and stronger, more empowered ports. At the dawn of the 21st century, as the region began to reawaken from economic doldrums and the effects of Asia's recession, the three ports joined in a new spirit of optimism and growth.

Vancouver has particularly prospered as a headquarters for global maritime interests. Attracted by the city, port and other incentives, maritime industry leaders are relocating to Vancouver. The most notable is Teekay Shipping, which has celebrated more than a decade in Vancouver. Founded by the late J. Torben Karlshoej, Teekay is a global leader in tanker shipping, moving approximately one-tenth of the world's oil.

The first decade of the 21st century sees Greater Vancouver achieving its destiny as a world-class urban centre, linked by land, air and especially by sea to global markets. Dramatic changes have, indeed, taken place

in the last few decades. An even greater transformation, however, may come within the near future. Soaring population and changes in transportation – new mass transit, new bridges and new roads – will potentially slow the movement of goods as more vehicles take to the roads. One possible solution might be a return to the water with smaller vessels using the Fraser River and Burrard Inlet as a means of bypassing traffic congestion. The pressures of ongoing urbanization will continue to provoke cities to demand more residential and commercial rather than industrial development along their waterfronts. But the economic lifeblood of the region, as well as the nation, depends on its ports and their facilities.

But while the landscape is altered, as new buildings arise and older ones fall, the surrounding waters will continue, essentially unchanged, ebbing and flowing off our shores. The sea and the mighty river, whose silt-laden fresh waters mingle with the Strait, shall remain ever-present – the same force that has drawn diverse peoples to our shores for millennia, from the first arrivals to our most recent immigrants. The waters will continue to sustain us with their harvests, as long as we manage them prudently, while they host our recreational pursuits, and their magnificent vistas refresh and renew our souls and inspire artistic creation. If we are to prosper, they will also continue to bring the commerce of the world to our doorstep.

Overleaf: This aerial view of Greater Vancouver, shows how the water defines the region – the Fraser River and its arms, the Strait, English Bay, Burrard Inlet and Howe Sound both surround and connect the communities with each other and with the outside world, as they have for centuries.

ACKNOWLEDGEMENTS

THE MARITIME HISTORY of Greater Vancouver has been the subject of many wonderful books and articles, and a wealth of unpublished materials. The pioneering research of Captain James Hamilton, Norman Hacking, W. Kaye Lamb, Leonard McCann and so many others paved the way for this book, as did some of the best maritime writing of the modern day, such as Doreen Armitage's superb history of Burrard Inlet. The maritime history of the Greater Vancouver region has been captured in the pages of *Harbour and Shipping* magazine for more than eight decades. The task of preparing this book was greatly aided by the meticulous work of the magazine through the years to capture as many stories and images as possible and to publish them. I am also grateful to publisher Murray McLellan and former editor Liz Bennett for their support when I worked as a columnist for *Harbour and Shipping* in the 1990s. I particularly want to thank William C. McKee, whose work on the maritime history of the area, especially the Port of Vancouver, has spanned the decades. Bill specially provided copies of his manuscript histories of Vancouver Harbour and the Pacific Rim he prepared for the Canadian Museum of Civilization, which were invaluable – as is the case with all of his work.

As always, I am indebted to the hard work of librarian and archivist Susan Buss of the Vancouver Maritime Museum's W.B. and M.H. Chung Library and the Leonard G. McCann Archives. Leonard McCann, curator emeritus, was another great help, as was S.C. Heal. Leonard's sleuthing and preliminary photo captioning made a nearly impossible task much easier. No one knows the visual record of the region's ports better than Len.

Information on the modern ports was provided with the usual professional aplomb and helpful support of the Fraser River Port Authority, through the offices of Raija Orava, Manager, Public Affairs, the North Fraser Port Authority, through the offices of Valerie A. Jones, Vice-President, Corporate Services and Corporate Secretary and the Vancouver Port Authority, through the offices of Ane McMullin, Director, Corporate communications and Public Affairs.

The text was reviewed by Jean Barman, Raija Orava, Valerie Jones, Leonard McCann, Ann Goodhart and Debbie Tardiff, and edited by Brian Scrivener.

Any errors or omissions are mine.

JAMES P. DELGADO
Vancouver, September 30, 2004

SOURCES

BOOKS

Armitage, Doreen. *Burrard Inlet: A History.* Madeira Park: Harbour Publishing, 2001.

Atamenenko, G.T., R.H. Fletcher, J.A. De Jong, J. Northey, and A.M. Strachan. *The Port of Vancouver: An Urban Planning Study.* Vancouver: Faculty of Graduate Studies, School of Community and Regional Planning, University of British Columbia, 1961.

Barr, Capt. James. *Ferry Across the Harbour – The Story of the North Vancouver Ferries.* Vancouver: Mitchell Press, 1969.

Bowsfield, Hartwell, ed., and Margaret A. Ormsby. *Fort Victoria Letters, 1846–1851.* Winnipeg: Hudson's Bay Record Society, 1979.

Burrows, James. *Port Watch: Historical Ships in Vancouver Harbour.* Vancouver: Vancouver City Archives, 1985.

Carver, John Arthur. *The Vancouver Rowing Club: A History, 1888–1980.* Vancouver: Aubrey F. Roberts, 1980.

Collier, Robert W., ed. *Symposium on the Port of Vancouver, June 20–24, 1966: Proceedings.* Vancouver: Department of Extension, University of British Columbia, 1966.

Corporation of the Harbour Commissioners of Vancouver. *By-Laws of the Corporation of the Harbour Commissioners of Vancouver, B.C., 1914.* Vancouver: Corporation of the Harbour Commissioners of Vancouver, 1914.

Cox, Thomas R. *Mills and Markets: A History of the Pacific Coast Lumber Industry to 1900.* Seattle and London: University of Washington Press, 1974.

Cutter, Donald C. *Malaspina and Galiano: Spanish Voyages to the Northwest Coast, 1791 & 1792.* Vancouver and Toronto: Douglas & McIntyre, 1991.

Davis, Chuck, ed. *The Greater Vancouver Book: An Urban Encyclopedia.* Surrey: Linkman Press, 1997.

Delgado, James P. *The Beaver: First Steamship on the West Coast.* Victoria: Horsdal & Schubart, 1993.

Delgado, James P. *Racers and Rovers: 100 Years of the Royal Vancouver Yacht Club.* Vancouver and Toronto: Douglas & McIntyre, 2003.

Fisher, Robin. *Vancouver's Voyage: Charting the Northwest Coast.* Vancouver and Toronto: Douglas & McIntyre, 1992.

Fisher, Robin and Hugh Johnston, eds. *From Maps to Metaphors: The Pacific World of George Vancouver.* Vancouver: University of British Columbia Press, 1993.

Gough, Barry. *The Royal Navy and the Northwest Coast of North America: 1810–1914.* Vancouver: University of British Columbia Press, 1971.

Gourley, Catherine. *Island in the Creek: The Granville Island Story.* Madeira Park: Harbour Publishing, 1988.

Graham, Donald. *Keepers of the Light: A History of British Columbia's Lighthouses and their Keepers.* Madeira Park: Harbour Publishing, 1985.

Gresko, Jacqueline and Richard Howard, eds. *Fraser Port: Freightway to the Pacific, 1858–1985.* Victoria: Sono Nis Press, 1986.

Hacking, Norman. *History of the Port of Vancouver.* Vancouver: Port of Vancouver, 1977.

Hacking, Norman. *The Two Barneys: A Nostalgic Memoir About Two Great British Columbia Seamen.* Vancouver: Gordon Soules Book Publishers Ltd., 1984.

Hagelund, William A. *Harbour Burning: A Century of Vancouver's Maritime Fires.* Surrey: Hancock House, 2002.

Hamilton, J.H., ed. *Vancouver Port Annual, British Columbia Ports and Western Canada Foreign Trade Directory, Second Edition.* Vancouver: Progress Publishing Company, 1930.

Hamilton, J.H. *Western Shores: Narratives of the Pacific Coast.* Vancouver: Progress Publishing, 1933.

Heal, S.C. *Conceived in War, Born in Peace: Canada's Deep Sea Merchant Marine.* Vancouver: Cordillera Publishing, 1992.

Hill-Turner, David. *Business in Great Waters: A Brief History of Pilotage in British Columbia Waters.* Vancouver: World Ship Society of British Columbia, 1987.

Johnston, Hugh. *The Voyage of the Komagata Maru: The Sikh Challenge to Canada's Colour Bar.* Vancouver: University of British Columbia Press, 1989.

Kendrick, John, and Robin Inglis. *Enlightened Voyages: Malaspina and Galiano on the Northwest Coast, 1791–1792.* Vancouver: Vancouver Maritime Museum, 1991.

Knight, Rolf. *Along the No. 20 Line: Reminiscences of the Vancouver Waterfront.* Vancouver: New Star Books, 1980.

Koppel, Tom. *Lost World: Rewriting Prehistory—How New Science is Tracing America's Ice Age Mariners.* New York: Atria Books, 2003.

Lamb, W. Kaye, ed. *The Voyage of George Vancouver, 1791–1795.* Four vols. London: Hakluyt Society, 1984.

Lamb, W. Kaye. *Empress to the Orient.* Vancouver: Vancouver Maritime Museum, 1991.

Lincoln, Leslie. *The Coast Salish Canoe.* Seattle: Center for Wooden Boats, 1991.

Lyon, Jim, and Barbara Duggan. *The Port of Vancouver: Canada's Global Gateway.* Vancouver: Vancouver Port Corporation/Douglas & McIntyre, 1993.

McCague, Fred, ed. *British Columbia Ports Handbook, Sea & Air Edition, 1996/97.* King's Lynn, Norfolk: Compass Publications, 1996.

MacDonald, Bruce. *Vancouver: A Visual History.* Vancouver: Talonbooks, 1992.

MacDonald, Robert A.J. *Making Vancouver: 1863–1913.* Vancouver: University of British Columbia Press, 1996.

McKee, William. *Portholes & Pilings: A Retrospective Look at the Development of Vancouver Harbour Up To 1933.* City of Vancouver Archives Occasional Paper #1. Vancouver: City Archives, 1978.

McLaren, Keith. *Light on the Water: Early Photography of Coastal British Columbia.* Vancouver and Toronto: Douglas & McIntyre, 1998.

McLaren, T.A., and Vickie Jensen. *Ships of Steel: A British Columbia Shipbuilder's Story.* Madeira Park: Harbour Publishing, 2000.

Manders, Valerie. *Portrait of Our Past: North Fraser Harbour Commission, 75th Anniversary.* Vancouver: North Fraser Harbour Commission, 1988.

Mansbridge, Francis. *Launching History: The Saga of Burrard Dry Dock.* Madeira Park: Harbour Publishing, 2002.

Marc, Jacques. *Historic Shipwrecks of Southern Vancouver Island.* Vancouver: Underwater Archaeological Society of British Columbia, 1990.

Matthews, Major J.S. *Early Vancouver: Narratives of Pioneers of Vancouver, B.C.* Two vols. Vancouver: Brock Webber Printing, 1959.

Moogk, Peter N. *Vancouver Defended: A History of the Men and Guns of the Lower Mainland Defences, 1859–1949.* Surrey: Antonson Publishing, 1978.

Morton, James. *The Enterprising Mr. Moody, the Bumptious Captain Stamp: The Lives and Colourful Times of Vancouver's Lumber Pioneers.* Vancouver: J.J. Douglas, 1977.

Perrault, Ernest G. *Wood & Water: The Story of Seaboard Lumber and Shipping.* Vancouver and Toronto: Douglas & McIntyre, 1985.

Reksten, Terry. *The Illustrated History of British Columbia.* Vancouver and Toronto: Douglas & McIntyre, 2001.

Rothery, Agnes. *The Ports of British Columbia.* Garden City, NJ: Doubleday, Doran, 1943.

Schreiner, John. *The Refiners: A Century of BC Sugar.* Vancouver and Toronto: Douglas & McIntyre, 1989.

Stacey, Duncan, and Susan Stacey. *Salmonopolis: The Steveston Story.* Madeira Park: Harbour Publishing, 1994.

Stevens, Robert White. *On the Stowage of Ships and their Cargoes: With Information Regarding Freights, Charter-Parties, &c. &c.* London: Longmans, Green, Reader, & Dyer, 1873.

Stone, David Leigh. *Vancouver's Undersea Heritage: Shipwrecks and Submerged Cultural Sites in Burrard Inlet and Howe Sound.* Vancouver: Underwater Archaeological Society of British Columbia.

Swankey, Ben, ed. *"Man Along the Shore!": The Story of the Vancouver Waterfront, As Told by the Longshoremen Themselves, 1860s–1975.* Vancouver: ILWU Local 500, 1975.

Swankey, Ben, ed. *A History of Shipbuilding in British Columbia As Told by Shipyard Workers.* Vancouver: Marine Retirees Association, 1977.

Taylor, G.W. *Timber: History of the Forest Industry in B.C.* Vancouver: J.J. Douglas, 1975.

Taylor, G.W. *Shipyards of British Columbia: The Principal Companies.* Victoria: Morriss Publishing, 1986.

Turner, Robert D. *The Pacific Princesses.* Victoria: Sono Nis Press, 1977.

Turner, Robert D. *The Pacific Empresses.* Victoria: Sono Nis Press, 1981.

Turner, Robert D. *Those Beautiful Coastal Liners: The Canadian Pacific's Princesses.* Victoria: Sono Nis Press, 2001.

Twigg, A.M. *Union Steamships Remembered, 1920–1958.* Campbell River: A.M. Twigg, 1997.

Walbran, Captain John T. *British Columbia Coast Names, 1592–1906. To Which Are Added a Few Names in Adjacent United States Territory, Their Origin and History.* Reprint ed. Vancouver and Toronto: Douglas & McIntyre, 1977.

Watts, Peter, and Tracy Marsh. *W. Watts & Sons, Boat Builders: Canadian Designs for Work and Pleasure, 1842–1946.* Oshawa, ON: Mackinaw Productions, 1997.

Wilbur, R. H.H. *Stevens, 1878–1973.* Toronto: University of Toronto Press, 1977.

Wynn, Graeme, and Timothy Oke, eds. *Vancouver and its Region.* Vancouver: University of British Columbia Press, 1992.

ARTICLES

Granberg, W.J. "Vancouver, Canada's Frontier Port." *Ships and the Sea* (May 1955), pp. 20–26.

Gunn, B.M. "The Design and Construction of Kaiser's Roberts Bank Coal Terminal." Paper presented at the 83rd Annual General Meeting of the Engineering Institute of Canada. Vancouver, September 12, 1969.

Hacking, Norman. "Steamboating on the Fraser in the Sixties." *British Columbia Historical Quarterly* (January 1946), pp. 1–4.

Howay, F.W. "Early Shipping in Burrard Inlet: 1863–1870." *British Columbia Historical Quarterly* (January 1937), pp. 3–20.

Keller, Betty. "By Sail and Steam to Vancouver." *The Beaver* (August/September 1987), pp. 28–34.

Stanton, John. "The Green Hill Park Disaster: A Memoir." *The Beaver* (April/May 1987), pp. 26–36.

Stevens, L. "The Grain Trade of the Port of Vancouver." *Economic Geography* (April 1936), pp. 185–96.

INDEX

A

Abyssinia 50, 51, 53, 80
Achilles 124, 125
Alaska 65, 72, 82, 166, 167
Alaska Cruise Line 168
Alaska cruise ships 145, 166–169
Alaska Marine Highway System 168
Alberta 94
Alberta Wheat Pool Elevator 94, 143
"All Red Route" 99
Allen, Doug 140
Allen, Joe 103
Allen, William 36
Allied Builders Ltd. 124
Allied Shipbuilders 124, 156, 157, 158, 160, 163
Amoco Cairo 143
Anian, Straits of (see Northwest Passage)
Annacis Island 152, 153, 157
APL Kennedy 145
Aquila 30
Armitage, Doreen 72
Arnold, John 9
Arnold 176 chronometer 9
Arrawac 100
Arrawac Charters Line 100
Asian seafarers, possibility of pre-European contact 5–6
Atta Boy 162
Australia, trade with 29, 43, 54, 98
Automobiles, trade in 153, 157

B

BC Coast Pilots 172
BC Ferries 150, 157, 160
BC Marine 84, 117
BC Marine Engineers 93
BC Sugar Refining Company 54, 58, 59, 163
B.C.P. 103 140
Baker, Joseph 10, 19
Ballantyne Pier 97, 103, 124, 134, 171
   Battle of 103
Barkley, Charles 8
Barzillai 29
Basford, Ron 163
Batavia 50, 53
Beaver 23, 26–27, 56, 70, 73
Benjamin Franklin 124
Blair Athole 58
Bodega y Quadra, Francisco 8

Boer War 82
Bowen Island 100, 123, 160
Bridges (also see Lions Gate Bridge and Second Narrows Bridge) 96, 97, 98
Brighton 33
British Columbia Pilotage Association 172
British Columbia Steamships Ltd. 113
British Ropes 85
Brockton Point 70, 73
Broughton, William 11
Buenos Aires 80
Burgess, Harry 58
Burns, Ken 104
Burrard Beaver 166
Burrard Dry Dock 93, 103, 113, 115, 116, 117, 118, 119, 122, 157, 158, 166
Burrard Grain Elevator 124
Burrard Inlet 1, 2, 4, 11, 16–17, 18, 23, 25, 26, 29, 35, 49, 50, 54, 61, 70, 71, 72, 74, 75, 82, 85, 89, 98, 130, 139, 143, 166, 172, 173, 177
Burrard Inlet Lumber Mills 29
Burrard Inlet Rowing Club 74
Burrard Inlet Sailing Club 74
Burrard Otter 166
Burt, Harry 133

C

C.H. Cates and Sons 158, 162, 166
Cadboro 15
Camsbusdoon 61
Camosun II 110
Campbell, Gordon 159
Canada Marine Act 177
Canada Place 97, 166, 169, 171
Canadian-Australian Steamship Company 54, 72, 122
Canadian Coast Guard 157
Canadian Fishing Company 40
Canadian Mortgage and Housing Corporation 163
Canadian National (CN) 98, 175
Canadian Northern 98
Canadian Pacific Navigation Company 65
Canadian Pacific Railway (CPR, CP) 40, 44, 45, 48, 49, 50, 53, 54, 55, 58, 61, 65, 66, 70, 71, 72, 75, 80, 87, 92, 93, 97, 98, 99, 109, 113, 157, 166, 167, 174, 175
Canadian Western Lumber 133
Canoes 2, 4, 12, 25
Canola oil, trade in 143
Carnival Cruise Lines 166, 169

Carnival Spirit 169
Cassiar 66
Catala 131, 134
Celebrity Cruises 166
Cellina 124
Centerm 30, 145, 166
Centennial Pier 134, 139, 148
Chatham, HMS 10, 11, 12
Chehalis 70, 72
Chelsea 30
Chestnut, Bill 149
China, trade with 50, 54, 94, 98, 143
Chisholm, Donna 171
City of New York 54
Clark, Glen 159
Clay, Harold 100
Clifford J. Rogers 126, 128-129, 144
Coal, trade in 18, 25, 87, 139, 144, 172, 174
Coal Harbour 18, 25, 50, 74, 93, 157, 158–159, 163
Coast Salish Canoe 4
Columbia River 15, 26
Columbus, Christopher 6
Collooney 18
Commodore 22
Containers (also see unitization) 124, 126, 130, 144, 148, 174, 175
Cook, James 8
Copper, trade in 98
Copper concentrates, trade in 139
Cosulich, Bob 133
Cosulich, Cecil 133
Cosulich, Norman 133
Cougar Ace 153
Coughlan, John 89
Coyle, Paddy 71
Crystal Cruises 166
Cutch 66

D

Deadman's Island 35
Deas, Joseph Sullivan 36
Deas Island 36, 157
Deighton, John "Gassy Jack" 33, 35
Delta 67
Deltaport 174, 175
Depression ("dirty thirties") 100, 102, 104, 162
Dillingham Corporation 162
Discovery, HMS 10, 11, 12, 19
Dolmage Towing 162
Dollarton Shipyard 158
Dominion Bridge Company 121

Domtar 162
Douglas, Sir James 18, 23
Drake, Sir Francis 6
Dredging 83
Drushka, Ken 162
Duke of Abercorn 44
Duncan, W. 148

E

Easthope, Ernest 157
Easthope, Ernie 157
Easthope, George 157
Easthope, Percy 157
Easthope, Vincent 157
Easthope Marine Engines 157
Effingham 80, 94
Ellen Lewis 29
Empress of Asia 55
Empress of China 54
Empress of India 48, 54, 56
Empress of Japan 54, 57, 58
Empress of Russia 108, 109
Empire Stevedoring Company 71, 149
English Bay 2, 11, 25, 29, 30, 31, 74, 82, 146, 166, 177
Enterprise 64, 65
Envoy 29
Expo 86 165, 169

F

Fairfield Island 5, 6
False Creek 2, 25, 61, 79, 82, 85, 89, 98, 120, 130, 133–134, 157, 163, 165
Farrington, Gordon 117, 118
"Fast Cats" 158–159, 160
Ferries, 33, 72, 75, 150, 157–160
Fertilizer, trade in 98, 143
Fireboats 120
Fish meal, trade in 98
Fish oils, trade in 36, 98
Flour, trade in 53, 81, 82, 95
Flying Dutchman 25
Fort Camosun 110
Fort Langley 15, 18, 23, 36
"Fort Steveston" 110, 113
Fort Vancouver 14, 15, 26
Fort Victoria 14, 18, 21
Fort Rae 113
Fraser River 2, 6, 12, 15, 16-17, 18, 22, 23, 25, 26, 35, 36, 64, 65, 67, 70, 72, 80, 82, 83, 100, 124, 130, 133, 138, 143, 144, 150, 151, 152, 153, 163, 165, 175, 177

Fraser River Discovery Centre 166, 172
Fraser River Pilots 172
Fraser River Port Authority 144, 150, 153, 165–166, 175, 177
Fraser Surrey Docks 152, 153, 175
Fraser Wharves Ltd. 153
Frazar and Company 50
Friedlander and Company 29
Frobisher, Martin 6

G

Galiano, Dionisio Alcalá 11, 12, 13
Game Over 140
"Gastown" 33
Genstar 162
Geraldine Wolvin 90
Gilbert, Humphrey 6
Glacier Queen 168
Glimpse 29
Gold Rushes
   California 18
   Fraser River 18, 22–23, 26, 35, 65, 66, 87
   Klondike 58, 66
Golden Arrow 148
Graham, Thomas Wilson 25
Grain, trade in 75, 79, 80, 82, 85, 89, 94, 97, 124, 143, 172
Grand Trunk Pacific Railroad 75, 98
Granville (town) 33, 35, 36, 49
Granville Island 82, 163–165
Granville Island Trust 163
Granville Street Bridge 61
Green Hill Park 120
Gresko, Jacqueline 153
Gulf of Georgia Cannery 77
Gulf of Georgia Towing Company 162

H

Hacking, Norman 103, 104
Haida 22
Hamilton, Captain James 89
Hanwell, Henry 15
Harbour and Shipping 126
Harbour Ferries 168
Hardcastle, Jack 105
Harris, Bob 171
Hastings Mill 33, 35, 38–39, 49, 72
Hattco Marine Services Ltd. 147
Heal, S.C. 121
Heaps Engineering 121
Henry Bay 171
Herring 36, 77, 98

Hobbs, J.W. "Joe" 102
Holland America 166
Hong Kong 94
Hood, HMS 115
Howard, Richard 153
Howay, F.W. 25
Hudsons Bay Company (HBC) 14, 15, 18, 22, 25, 26, 64, 65
Hume, Fred J. 133

I

I-26 110
Imperial Munitions Board 89
Imperial Oil 122, 175
Industrial Workers of the World (IWA) 71
International Longshoremens Association (ILA) 71, 103
Ireland, Moses 32
Irving, John 65
Irving, William 65
Isabel 33
Island Tug and Barge 162
Islander 65

J

J.H. Carlisle 120
J.R. MacDonald 66
Jade Forest 160
Japan 5
   Drifting seafarers 5
   Trade with 44, 50, 53, 54, 94, 98, 143, 144, 153, 157, 170
Japanese-Canadians, wartime relocation and internment 110–112
Jensen, Vickie 171
Jericho 30
Joe, Chief Philip 12
Johansen, Gina 171
John Coughlan and Sons 89, 93, 164
Johnson, B.D.L. "Barney" 139, 144, 148
Johnson, E. Pauline (Tekahionawake) 176
Johnston, Hugh 87
Johnston, Lucille 172
Jones, Harold 162
Jones, Harold Jr. 162
Jones, William 70
Juneau 65, 167

K

Kaiser Resources 144
Keast, Howard 130
Kent 29
Ketchikan 65

Kingcombe Navigation 162
Kitsilano Indian Reserve 79
Knight, Rolf 103, 163
Knights of Labour 71
Komagata Maru 86–87
Kruzik, Alice 117–118
Kuroshio ("black current") 5

L

Labouchere 65
Lady Alexandra 123, 156
Lady Cecilia 123
Lady Jean 156
Lady Joyce 156
Lady Lisbeth 156
Lady Vivien 156
La Belle 162
La Mars 162
La Mite 130
La Reine 162
LaPointe Pier 118, 139
Lamb, W. Kaye 53
Lead, trade in 98
Leonora 33, 66
Le Roi 162
Liberty Ace 153
Lighthouses 70
Lincoln, Leslie 4
Lindsay, Arthur 162
Linton, Andy 61, 74
Lions Gate 1, 72, 94, 109
Lions Gate Bridge 109, 113, 120, 132
Lok, Michael 8
Longshoremen 71, 81, 95, 103, 149–150
Lonsdale Quay 157, 166
Looe, William J. 30
Lorne 96, 97
Lumber, trade in 18, 25, 28–30, 33, 38–39, 40, 53, 71, 150
Lyall, William 93
Lynnterm 148

M

McCandless, Alexander 80
McCarter, Nairne, and Partners 102
McDonald, Evelyn Pearce 116
McDonald, Stan 169
McEwan, Doris 117
McKee, William 61, 71, 98
McKenzie, Alexander "Sandy" 146–147
McKenzie, Dave 147
McLaren, T. Arthur 122, 124, 157
McLaren, W.D. 121

MacLean, Alexander 6
McPhail, Joy 159
McPherson, Donald 130
Mabel Brown 89, 90, 91
Marcia 74
Marega, Charles 132
Marine Building (Vancouver) 102
Maritime fur trade 12, 15, 18
Martinez, Jimmy 118
Massey Tunnel 150
Mastodon 83
Matsumoto, Ichijuro "Phillip" 158
Matsumoto, Isumo "Sam" 158
Matsumoto, Ken 158
Matsumoto Shipyards 157–158
Matthews, Major J.S. 6
Mechanization, effects of 149–150
Menchions Shipyard 147, 163
Menchions, William R. 163
Menestheus 121
Mercer Brothers 101
Metropolis 29
Mexicana 12, 13
Mexico, trade with 29, 82
Miowera 54
Miranda, Louis 12
Montcalm 92
Moody, Richard 23, 44
Moody, Sewell P. "Sue" 28, 29–30, 32, 33, 35, 139
Moogk, Peter 113
Moodyville 28, 29, 33
Morayshire 58
Morton, John 25
Murray, Bill 103
Musqueam 2, 17, 35

N

Nanaimo 18, 25, 26, 66, 105, 172
Narváez, José Maria 11
National Harbours Board 104, 139
Naval Examination Service 109, 112-113
Neptune Bulk Terminals 139, 142, 143
New Westminster 23, 25, 29, 35-36, 64, 65, 66, 70, 75, 80, 82, 94, 100, 150, 152, 153, 165
New Westminster Construction Company 93
New Westminster Harbour Commissioners 150, 153
New Westminster Quay 165, 166
New Zealand, trade with 80, 94
Nippon Kokan K.K. 144

Nissan Motors 153
Nootka 8, 11
North Fraser (North Arm) 82, 83, 130, 144, 165, 175
North Fraser Port Authority 165, 175, 177
North Fraser Port Commissioners 83
North Vancouver 71, 75, 93, 97, 98, 156, 157, 162, 163
North Vancouver 75
North Vancouver Ferry No. 2 75
North Van Ship Repairs 117, 118, 121, 122
North West Cruise Ship Association 166
Northland Prince 160
Norvan 75
Norwegian Cruise Line 166
Northwest Passage 6, 8, 43, 93

O
Ocean Cement 163
On Time 162
Orea No. 1 141
Oriental and Occidental Line 53
Orpheus 32
Otter 22, 65

P
Pacific 32
Pacific Coast Bulk Terminal 139
Pacific Coast Steamship Company 72
Pacific Coast Terminals (New Westminster) 150, 153
Pacific Construction 93
Pacific Elevators 153
Pacific Gatherer 96, 97
Pacific Mail Steamship Company 53
Pacific Pilotage Authority 172
Pacific Tanker Company 162
Panama Canal 75, 79, 85, 89, 94
Paper, trade in 98, 122, 130, 139, 175
Parthia 50, 53
Parthia Shoal 49, 83
Pender, Daniel 26
Perez, Juan 8
Peru, trade with 29
Philippines, trade with 82, 94
Phillipson, Cathie 147
Phillipson, Clem 147
Phillipson, Jim 147
Phosphate rock, trade in 143
Pier B-C 97, 166
Pier D fire 120
Pilots 29, 33, 172
Pioneer Line 65

Pioneer Mills 25
Point Atkinson 17, 35, 70, 73
Plumper, HMS 25
Point Grey 11, 17, 25, 109, 133
Point Roberts 150
Potash, trade in 139, 143
Port Moody 44, 45-46, 49, 122, 139
Pretty, Charles 79
Prince Rupert 75, 94
Princess Cruises 166, 169
Princess Kathleen 167
Princess Louise 93, 167
Princess Marguerite 113, 169
Princess Patricia 113, 169
Princess Victoria 66, 70
Progressive Engineering 121
Prospect Point 27, 34, 56, 70, 73, 83, 109
Prospect Point Signal Station 83
Ptolemy, Claudius 3
Puget, Peter 11, 12
Puget Sound 17, 30, 53, 153
Pulp, trade in 98, 122, 130, 133, 139, 148, 175

Q
Queen Charlotte Islands 22

R
R.P. Rithet 64
Radisson Seven Seas Cruises 171
Rainbow, HMCS 86, 87
Rance, Lilian Matheson 116
Rankin, Jonnie 117
Recreational boating 74
Red Fir No. 1 133
Richards, George Henry 17, 25
River Towing Company 133
Rivtow 133, 172
Robert Allan Ltd. 120, 160
Roberts Bank 144, 174
Rogers, Benjamin Tingley "B.T." 54
Rogers, Jeremiah "Jerry" 30
Rowlings, J.H. 36
Royal Canadian Engineers 109
Royal Canadian Mounted Police (RCMP) 97, 103, 104
Royal Canadian Navy 112, 121
Royal Caribbean International 166
Royal Engineers 23
Royal Navy (UK) 23, 25, 26, 44, 121
Royal Vancouver Yacht Club 74
Russia: Interest, Exploration 8, 15

S
St. Mongo No. II 141
St. Roch 93, 114, 115
Salish, Coast 4
Salmon 18, 34, 36, 72, 75, 76, 98, 138
Saltwater Women at Work 172
Samson V 166
Sandheads No. 16 70
San Juan 141
Santa Saturnina 11
San Francisco (also see United States) 18, 22, 29, 32, 33, 35, 72
Saskatchewan Wheat Pool Elevator 142, 143
Sawmills 18, 25, 29, 30, 35, 40, 61, 130, 153, 165
Seaboard Shipping 122
Seaboard Terminal 143
Seabus 166
Seaforth Highlanders 87
Seaspan (Cyprus) Ltd. 160
Seaspan International 162, 177
Seaspan Offshore Group 160
Seattle 58, 65, 74, 144, 153, 167, 169
Sea Foam 33
Sea Lion 87
Sea otter pelts, trade in 8, 15
Second Narrows Bridge (first) 96, 97
    Second bridge 98
    Third bridge (Ironworkers' Memorial) 134, 135
Senator 66, 72
Senor 74
Shipbuilding
    Depression 102-103
    First World War 88-93, 164
    Second World War 109, 116-119, 121-122
    Post-Second World War 122, 124, 157, 158-161
    Women involved in 116, 117-118
Silk, trade in 43, 50, 52, 54
"Silk train" 54
Simpson, Aemilius 15
Simpson, Sir George 14
Sitka 65
Siwash Rock (S'i'lix) 109, 176
Skagway 130, 167
Skidegate 66
skid roads 30, 31
Smit Marine Canada 133, 172, 177
Smith, Bill "Spider" 149
Smith, Hec 100

South Sand Heads 66
Spain: Interest, exploration 8, 11, 12, 13, 17
Spratt, Joseph 36, 40
Spratt's Ark 36, 40
"Spratt's Oilery" 36
Squamish Nation 2, 4, 11, 12, 17, 25, 35, 71, 176
Stalker, Hugh 72
Stamp, Edward 30, 33, 36
Stamp's Mill 30, 33, 35, 36
Stanley Park 25, 57, 73, 74, 109, 112, 132, 166
Star Grindanger 148
Star Shipyards 101
Stella Fortune 162
Stenna Lines 113
Stevedores 95
Stevens, Henry Herbert 82
"Stevens' Folly" 85, 89, 94
Steveston 66, 70, 72, 75, 110, 112
Stewart, Jim 162
Straits Brothers 133
Sugar, trade in 54, 58, 59, 61
Sullivan, Josephine and Phillip 35
Sulphur, trade in 139, 172
Susan Sturgis 22
Sutherland, Robin 149
Sutil 12, 13

T
Takaya 160
Taylor, A.J.T. 132
Tea, trade in 44, 45, 46-47, 50
Teekay Shipping 177
Terminal Systems Inc. (TSI) 128, 174
Terra Nova 141
Thomas F. Bayard 70
Thomas, Jack "Navvy Jack" 33
Tilbury Island 150
Timms, Carl 44
Todd, Gertie 116
Trans Mountain Pipe 172
Trott, Edward 74
Tseil-waututh 2, 17, 35
Turpin, Charles 85
Twigg, Art 110
Tymac Launch Service 146-147, 171
Tymac 146
Tymac No. 2 146
Tymac No. 3 146
Tymac No. 4 147
Tyson, Sam 146

U

Underwater Archaeological
  Society of BC 27
Union ("Sudden Jerk") 72
Union Steam Ship Company 33, 66, 67,
  72, 100, 131, 134, 166
United States of America: Interests,
  exploration, trade 12, 15, 18, 21
  (also see San Francisco)
Unitization (also see containers) 124, 126
University of British Columbia 134, 144

V

Valdés, Cayetano 11, 12, 13
Valerianos, Apostolos (Juan de Fuca) 8
Van Bramer, James 32, 33
Van Horne, William 49
Vancouver (includes port of) 40, 41, 49,
  50, 53, 54, 58, 61, 65, 66, 70, 72, 74, 75,
  79, 80, 82, 85, 93, 94, 97, 98, 100, 102,
  103, 104, 109, 110, 112, 115, 120, 130, 132,
  133–134, 138, 139, 143, 144, 145, 146,
  148, 157, 158, 162, 163, 164, 165, 166,
  168, 169, 170, 172, 171, 173, 175, 177
Vancouver Barge Transportation 162
Vancouver Board of Trade 80
Vancouver Engineering Works 121
Vancouver Fireboat No. 2 120
Vancouver Granite Company 164
Vancouver Iron Works 121
Vancouver Island 6, 14, 18, 22, 25, 49
Vancouver Lumber Company 164
Vancouver Maritime Museum 6, 57,
  114, 115
Vancouver Port Authority 175, 177
Vancouver Port Corporation 144, 148,
  150, 166
Vancouver Rowing Club 74
Vancouver Shipyards 93, 158, 160, 162
Vancouver Tug Boat Company 162
Vancouver Wharves 139
Vancouver Yacht Club 74
Vancouver, George 9, 10, 11, 12, 13, 17, 19
Vanisle Tug and Barge 162
Vanterm 148
Venture (2) 67, 68
Versatile Pacific 157, 160
Victoria 22, 25, 29, 58, 64, 65, 72, 93,
  122, 167, 172
Victoria and Vancouver Stevedoring
  Company 71

W

W.B. Flint 44, 45, 46–47
Wade, F.C. 80
Walkem, G.A. 121
Wallace, Alfred 61, 89, 93, 117
Wallace, Clarence 117
Walters, Harry 71
War Dog 89
War Power 89
War Storm 89
Washington Marine Group of
  Companies 158, 159, 160, 162
Watts, William 74, 93
West, Chuck 168
West Coast Shipbuilders 117, 188, 121,
  122, 124
West Vancouver 33, 75
Western Bridge and Steel 121
Western Canada Shipyard 90, 93
Western Canada Steamship Company 122
Western Tug and Barge 162
Westland Iron and Steel Foundry 121
Westminster Iron Works 121
White Pass and Yukon 126, 129, 144, 167
Whitehorse 167
William and Ann 15
William Dollar 96, 97
World Explorer Cruises 166
World War, First 89, 92, 93, 107
World War, Second 109–114, 116–122

Y

Yarrows 122
Yosemite 27
Yukon Star 168

Z

Zinc, trade in 98

CREDITS AND PERMISSIONS

EVERY REASONABLE EFFORT has been made to trace and contact all holders of copyright and to credit sources correctly. In the event of omission or error SA&D Publishers should be notified so that a full acknowledgment may be made in future editions.

Unless specified otherwise, all artifacts and photographs, are from the Vancouver Maritime Museum collections. Most of the Museum's exceptional artworks come from the Mary and Bill Everett Family Collection.

BC Archives:
p.23, PDP 01891.

Canadian Pacific Railway Archives
p.45 NS-19991; p.99 right, A-6024;
p.99 left, A.C. Leighton, A-6701.

Canadian Press
p.170, C. Stoody, 1166404.

City of Vancouver Archives
p.31, LOG P3N4; p.36, BU P42;
p.41, H.T. Devine, LGN 453;
p.85, J.A. Brook, CAN P11.

Library and Archives Canada
p.3, NMC 019268; p.10, NMC 135094;
p.15, C 4219; p.24, C 037867;
p.111, PA 37486; p.119 bottom,
E 00061864; p.138, C 010340.

P. Martin-Morice
p.165.

K. Meyer
p.27 bottom left, 57 top left, 115 left,
131 bottom right.

North Vancouver Museum and Archives
p.89, 27-2669; p.116, 8108; p.117, 27-295;
p.119 top, 27-2780.

New Westminster Public Library
p.29, 48.

Oregon Historical Society
p.13, 097867.

Vancouver Public Library,
Special Collections
p.74, 2891; p.87, 6229; p.94, 2829;
p.96, 3114; p.98, 6462; p.104, 8829;
p.112, 3191; p.164 right, L. Frank, 10645;
left , L. Frank, 3675.

Vancouver Museum
p.4, 1140.

The following corporations and individuals generously provided images from their archives and collections.

Allied Shipbuilders
p.118, 121, 156, 164.

Atkins & Doull (Feckless Collection)
p. frontispiece, title page, contents page,
1, 7, 20, 34, 42, 62–63, 78, 84, 106, 137,
136, 154–155, 176.

BC Sugar
p.59, 61.

Canadian Pacific Railway Archives
p.174, R. Robinson, E-8191-16.

Fraser River Port Authority
p.101, 128, 148 left, 149, 150, 151, 152,
153, 175.

McElhanney Consulting Services
p.178–179.

R.V. Stevenson
p.109.

Tymac Launch Service
p.146, 147.

Vancouver Port Authority
p.145, 148 right, 169, 173, 180.

Vickie Jensen
p.171.

Washington Marine Group
p.142, 161, 162.

THIS BOOK was inspired by a collection of local maritime prints assembled over the last twenty years by my wife, Barbara, and myself, with the collaboration of our friend Bob Doull.

Since 1998, the prints have been housed in a studio in a renovated industrial building at the north end of Gore Street, just where the railway defines the border between the land and the working harbour. The sight of bright orange cranes loading cargo ships and fishing boats unloading their catch, the continued raucous call of the gulls, and the loud coupling of box cars are a natural frame for a collection of lively waterfront images.

The idea of a book based on the print collection started five years ago and evolved until it became the book you are now holding. Over that period several people encouraged me, for which I am particularly grateful: Scott McIntyre, Celia Duthie and Nick Hunt, Robin Wall, Mark Stanton and Roberto Dosil. To them I would like to say thank you. As you can see, I was listening. Your advice is evident in this volume.

DON ATKINS
Vancouver, February 15, 2005

Stanton Atkins & **Dosil** Publishers
Mailing address:
2632 Bronte Drive
North Vancouver, BC
Canada V7H 1M4

National Library of Canada Cataloguing in Publication

Delgado, James P.,
Waterfront: The Illustrated Maritime Story of Greater Vancouver

Includes bibliographical references and index
ISBN 0-9732346-5-2

SA&D Publishers would like to thank the following people, for their contributions to the project, Katherine Bamford, Susan Buss, Mark Erdman, Robin Inglis, Jennifer Jones, Robert Kennell, Francis Mansbridge, Malcolm McLaren, Megan Park, Cathie and Jim Phillipson, Marilyn Sacks, R.V. Stevenson, Debbie Tardiff, Daniel Tresa, the staff at the Vancouver Maritime Museum and a special thank you to Leonard McCann, for his patience and for sharing his knowledge while we searched through the Museum's images and artifacts collections.

Edited by: Brian Scrivener
Designed by: Roberto Dosil
Principal photography by: Bruce Law
Printed by: C&C

This book's text, sidebars and captions are set in Quadraat Regular and Quadraat Sans, a typeface family designed by Fred Smeijers in 1992. The titles are set in Trade Gothic, a typeface originally designed by Jackson Burke in 1948.